THE ECONOMY OF
A SOUTH INDIAN TEMPLE

THE ECONOMY OF A SOUTH INDIAN TEMPLE

V. G. RAMAKRISHNA IYER

GYAN

Published by

Gyan Publishing House
5, Ansari Road
Daryaganj, New Delhi-110002
Phone: 011-47034999, 9811692060
E-mail: books@gyanbooks.com

Distribution Network
gyanbooks.com
India, USA, Canada, UK, Australia

ISBN: 978-93-7447-030-5 (PB)

First Published, 1946

2nd Impression 2025

Printed at: Gyan Press, Delhi.

THE ECONOMY OF A SOUTH INDIAN TEMPLE
Author: V. G. RAMAKRISHNA IYER

THE ECONOMY OF A
SOUTH INDIAN TEMPLE

(Sankara Parvati Prize Essay of the Madras University)

BY

V G RAMAKRISHNA AIYER, M A

Reader in Economics Annamalai University

PUBLISHED BY THE ANNAMALAI UNIVERSITY

ANNAMALAINAGAR

1946

CONTENTS

ABBREVIATIONS USED IN THE TEXT

A. R. E.	Annual Report on Epigraphy (Madras).
E. I.	Epigraphia Indica
J. O. R	Journal of Oriental Research
S. I. I.	South Indian Inscriptions

THE
ECONOMY OF A SOUTH INDIAN TEMPLE

CHAPTER I

I

INTRODUCTION

South India is a land of temples These temples supply the data by which we may reconstruct to some extent the ancient annals and recall to life the morality, the literature, the politics and the art of the past The numerous inscriptions of South India are found engraved on temple walls, and some of the great achievements of South Indian kingdoms are revealed by these inscriptions Inscriptions are almost the only contemporary record for the various periods to which they relate These inscriptions are mostly either on stone or metal Their primary object is in general to record the erection of temples or other public structures the endowment to gods or Brahmans with land and gifts or to commemorate acts of heroisms or self-sacrifice But we also learn about the ruling powers of the day, their achievements and other information useful for historical purposes To arrive at a just conception of the past annals there is nothing better than these inscriptions, and to combine the details of the epigraphic material into a consecutive narrative would add to our knowledge and correct previous misconceptions of some historical events The mediaeval period of South

Indian history was an age of temple building, an the religious edifices all over South India ar standing monuments of the achievements of th rulers of the time.

That temples have existed in South India fron very early times is evident from Sangam literature The earliest epigraphical record of the existence of temples takes us back to the age of the Pallava kings between the fourth and the ninth centuries A. D. While the earliest temples were built probably of wood and other perishable material, stone temples came into existence in South India with the Pallavas The Cholas who succeeded the Pallavas are very well-known as the greatest temple-builders of Southern India. Almost all the big temples of South India were built by mediaeval South Indian rulers

The temple was also the place where ancient kings performed their tūlabhāra ceremonies which attracted crowds of people from all parts of the kingdom. The Pandya king Sundara Pandya is said to have performed his tūlabhāra at Chidambaram. In almost all the temples visited by South Indian kings special festivals called after their names were ordered to be conducted annually on the asterism of their birth day, and rich endowments were made for them. Offerings were made to the temple sometimes to secure merit for the dead, or to get success in a field of a battle or to be rid of sickness from which one was suffering or for obtaining prosperity, wealth and happiness in life.

should govern the architecture of the temple.[1] The temples of India with their images and rituals, their bathing tanks and offerings of fruits and flowers, with their pillars, domes and spires are essentially a product of Indian thought and Indian social and economic conditions. The more attractive story of Indian thought as expressed in religion and philosophy, literature and art is as important as dynastic history for an intelligent understanding of South Indian contribution to Indian culture. To the student of South Indian history and antiquities, the temple is therefore a most important institution.

Before proceeding to deal with the history of Chidambaram temple, it is well to indicate the importance of the study of temple history by reference to some general aspects of the South Indian temple.

II

SOME ASPECTS OF THE SOUTH INDIAN TEMPLE

The numerous temples all over South India are a constant attraction to the study of local history. There is scarcely a village of reasonable size without a temple. According to the Hindu conception, no village is complete without a temple of its own. These temples have played an important part in the religious, social and economic life of the people Almost all the big temples were

1. Sukranītisāra Vol 13. Sacred Books of the East, pp. 166-182.

constructed by kings or rulers, in some cases as mark of their religious devotion, and sometimes in commemoration of their military glory. The South Indian temples with their life and polity were essentially religious institutions They were also a powerful social and economic entity. The temples were corporations founded with the full co-operation of the local public; and they enjoyed a very large and devoted patronage from the ruling kings and their subordinates They were common both to the ruler and the ruled enjoying the fullest advantages of their healthy co-operation. There were various forms of royal patronage to the temples, such as the giving of villages or lands for the benefit of the temple, making over to the temples the taxes due to the state[1]; and remitting taxes on lands gifted away to the temples by various donors.[2]

From some of the inscriptions we are able to glean information about the political conditions of the times. Political compacts were sometimes engraved on temple walls.[3] An inscription[4] in the Viṣṇu temple in Tiruvendipuram dated in the 16th year of Rājarāja III (1231-32) contains an interesting account of certain political disturbances which happened in Southern India. It states that King Perunjinga had captured the Cōla Emperor, apparently Rājarāja III, at Sēndamangalam and the Hoysala King Narasimha II seized Perunjinga with

1. A. R. E 270 of 1921-22; Appendix B.
2. A. R. E. 349 of 1921-22; Appendix B.
3 A. R. E. 107 of 1900 and 115 of 190.

his wives and treasures and reinstated the Chōla Empeior. It also stated that Parākramabāhu, King of Ceylon, who seems to have been allied to Perunjinga, lost his life in the course of the war. There are also several epigraphs which refer to political compacts by the royal chieftains to safeguard their life, power and prestige. These compacts seem to indicate that places far away from the seat of the Central Government were in a state of political unrest[a] From some of the instances of political compacts; we may say that they were formed generally in South India with the cognizance of of the king to fix the boundaries of the territories of the contracting parties, and to safeguard them against aggression, to enable petty chieftains to present a united front in time of stress and to express vows of fealty to the king or the ruling chiefs Some of the temples have occasionally served as forts against external invaders.

Occasionally the safety of the temples and their property seems to have been guaranteed in ancient times by precautionary measures, *i e.* by placing them under the protection of guards. An inscription[2] at Saṅgramanallūr (Coimbatore district) states that the gōpura, the temple and its priests were placed under the protection of soldiers. Another record[3] from Tiruvālīśvaram (Tinnevelly district) states that the local temple, its treasury and the temple servants were placed under the

---

1. A R. E. 55 of 1929
2. A R E 167 of 1909.
3. A. R. E 120 of 1905.

protection of the Chōla army called Mūnrukai-mahāsēnai. Interest was also evinced by the Perumpadaiyar and Valangai-mahā-sēnaiyar in the affairs of the temple at Perungulam[1] (Tinnevelly district).

Temple control:—The duty of supervising the temple administration seems to have been entrusted to a Committee of the assembly itself appointed every year or to independent bodies subject to the control of the assembly. Generally every temple was in the management of a Committee. In cases where there was no particular committee for this purpose, the village assembly acted as the trustee for the charities connected with the temple.[2] Temple lands and charities were not all as a rule in the hands of some managers. There were cases in which money meant for certain services in the temple was left in the custody of the priests (Vaikānasa) of the temple.[3] There were instances where such recipients proved delinquent, and compensation in land or money was recovered from them by the King or his officers

Temple Treasury:—There were elaborate provisions for the management of the temple accounts. Where the temple treasury was in charge of a Committee, the Committee was not a merely receiving and disbursing body, but possessed also administrative powers like the selling of the temple land on suitable conditions.[4] The surplus in the temple

---

1 A R E 1932-33 p 68.
2 A. R. E. 343 and 349 of 1921–22; Appendix B
3. A. R. E 318 of 1921 22, Appendix B
4. A. R. E 321 of 1921-22, Appendix B

treasury was in some cases utilised for special purposes either with the consent or at the instance of the local village assembly.[1] The temple bought and sold lands as necessary like any property owner and kept strict accounts of its assets and liabilities An interesting record of the 17th year of Rajaraja I states that royal officers inquired into the management of temple lands and expenses There were cases of embezzlement and inquiry by a royal commission in Chōla times, There were also instances of honest management and accountancy, An epigraph[2] from Tirukōyilur relates that the temple committee recovered from a Śrivaisnava Brahman ten cows on the evidence of an entry in the temple accounts that his grandfather had received ten cows from a chief named Pirudigangan, for the purpose of supplying curds for Brahmins fed in a Matha

The temple, whenever necessary, farmed out or commuted its revenue[3] and leased out its lands perpetually to private individuals, receiving reasonable advance payment and agreeing to receive a certain amount annually thereafter[4] It transferred at will, if necessary, the obligations previously set upon one class of people to another,[5] while in a few other cases, the communal maintenance of the charity was agreed upon in spite of odds[6] The

---

1 A R E 208 of 1921 22 Appendix B
2 A R E 327 of 1921 22
3 A R E. 201 of 1921 22 Appendix B
4 A R E 321 and 325 of 1921 22 Appendix B
5 A R E 281 of 1921 22 Appendix B
6 A R E 263 of 1921 22 Appendix B

temple inscriptions served as a permanent record for all time, and whenever there was a renovation of the temple, these inscriptions were re-engraved under official supervision.[1] The temple authorities besides looking after the temple affairs attended to the feeding of ascetics and pilgrims.

A record of the time of Sundara Pāṇḍya[2] gives an instance of how the trustees acted when the dues on temple lands fell into arrears. In this inscription from Kāṭṭumannārkōil (Chidambaram taluk), it is stated that the trustees of the temples situated between the rivers Koḷḷiḍam and Veḷḷāṟu came to an agreement and decided to remit the dues on lands given for worship and offerings to the temple at Chidambaram and that the amount should be rateably enhanced on the remaining lands in the village so as to recoup the amount remitted. There are records of grants of lands made to private individuals for definite services rendered, *viz.* for the finishing up and construction of a temple tank and well[3] for the polishing of the images of gods.[4] This system of giving lands for services offers a strange contrast to the modern practice of payment in money. The gift of land which served as a permanent source of income must have been intended as a remuneration made for the benefit of the temple on behalf of which the grants were made. Apart from such gifts of lands for services rendered, there are also instances of

1. A. R. E. 486 and 487 of 1921-22, Appendix B
2. A. R. E. 535 of 1920
3. A. R. E. 37 of 1920.
4. A. R. E. 338 of 1920.

of communal gifts on behalf of temples. An inscription[1] dated in Saka 1199 registers the conferring of a holding 'vritti' on a smith by the temple servants.

The economy of the temple:—The temples have played an important part in the economic life of the people. Every big temple has been a wealthy institution owning vast properties in land. As the biggest landlord, the temples have employed a large number of labourers. They have culivated lands, besides encouraging rural activities like extension of cultivation and rehabilitation of villages. Every temple has been a huge consumer and has purchased various articles for purposes of conducting worship The temples were generally wealthy and the wealth of the South Indian temples was a wonder to foreign travellers in mediaeval times The wealth of the temples was made of royal endowments, and benefactions by the public. Endowments were usually known as dēvadāya or dēvadāna lands The kings patronised temples by either making grants of lands tax-free or at low quit-rent to be enjoyed by them in perpetuity, or by making over specified taxes of their area in which the temple was situated. Endowments were also made for specific purposes, as for the repair of a portion of the temple or the institution of a service in the name of the donor. Costly jewellery was presented to the temples and provisions were made for some services by the dedication of cow and sheep. An epigraph[2] refers

1. A. R E 729 of 1920
2. A R. E 267 of 1891

to an endowment for the provision of tuḷasi leaves to a temple. Numerous endowments refer to the provision for flower garden or 'nandavanams.' The 'sarvamānya' grant to a temple shows the absolute ownership it could exercise on the land. An interesting epigraph of Krishnadēva Rāya[1] shows that he remitted 10,000 'varāhas' in favour of a large number of temples in the Chōla mandalam. The temples were allowed to collect the taxes for their maintenance and repair. From the economic point of view, the temple was a big land-lord owning properties got by gifts and also by purchase with the surplus funds. The temples also protected the interests of the tenants who cultivated their lands.[2] Also the temples played an important part in the reclamation of waste lands[3]; sometimes the temple lands were sold to meet the expenses of the repair of tanks.[4] For the worship of the temple many articles were in demand—cocoanut, sandal, rice, camphor, ghee, sugar, leaves, flowers etc. The temple provided work for a good number of people.[5] The part played by the temple servants in the economy of the temple is attested by several epigraphs.[6] The temple served as a means of rendering relief to the poor. The temples were the principal feeding houses of the locality; strangers, ascetics, men of learning were fed sumptuously in the

1. A. R. E 74 of 1903
2. A. R. E 226 of 1913—Report para 54.
3. A. R. E 258 of 1910.
4. A. R. E. 251 of 1906.
5. Elliot—History of India, IV, 105.
6. A. R. E. 415 of 1912, 239 of 1912, 347 of 1912, 270 of 1916 E. I. IV, p. 90.

temples and on festive occasions a large number of poor people were fed. Some of the temples also maintained hospitals.[1] The claims of hereditary officers were settled by a Sābha.[2] The principle followed in regard to appointment to offices in temples, remuneration[3] of servants, and service inams[4] is attested by several inscriptions Small industries *e.g.* weaving were encouraged.[5]

There are instances of rich temples supporting poor ones An epigraph[6] is of interest as showing how small temples which were not very prosperous were helped by the richer ones It states that the Mahēśvaras and the Tānattar (sthānikās) of the temple of Rāmānandīśvara at Tirukaṇṇapuram approached the temple authorities at Chidambaram in their assembly hall and represented to them that the income of the temple was insufficient. Those assembled in the hall resolved therefore that in the districts within the influence of the temple, all the servants of the Śiva temples should make a contribution

There are several inscriptions to show that persons misappropriating temple property (śivadrōhins) were severly punished. The commission of sin against temples was tantamount to treason and the offenders were punished by exilement and

1. E. I. Vol. IV p. 90.
2 A. R. E. 576 of 1916
3. S. I. I. II, 256.
4. A R. E. 193 of 1916.
5. A. R. E 368 of 1923, 370 of 1923 and 381 of 1923.
6. A. R. E. 537 of 1922.

confiscation of property. The property of Śiva drōhins did not escheat to the king, but was invariably made over to the temple.[1] One of these records[2] registers a royal order assigning the proceeds of the sale of certain rights in the temple worship and of the sale of the tenancy rights over the temple lands confiscated from certain Śivabrāhmanas who had stolen gold from the temple treasury, for the benefit of the temple. How Śivadrōhins and Rājadrōhins were dealt with are clearly brought out by a number of inscriptions, notably the three inscriptions of the time of Rājarāja III.[3] An inscription[4] records a royal order to the authorities of the temple (Tirunāgēśvaram) sanctiong the auction sale of the lands and rights belonging to two temple accountants who had embezzled some money from the temple treasury and thus committed Śivadrōha.

Several instances of the formation of agrahāras and villages have been mentioned in the inscriptions of the temples; and we learn from them that facilities were afforded by kings to encourage such settlements, and that certain initial concessions in the matter of taxes were also generally granted to the colonists to enable them to bring the land under efficient cultivation in easy stages.[5]

---

1. A. R. E. 115 of 1932; 189 of 1929.
2. A. R. E. 115 of 1932.
3. A. R. E. 225, 279 and 303 of 1927.
4. A. R. E. 70 of 1932.
5. A. R. E. 78 of 1929.

Though the construction of temples and the provision for worship therein by grants of lands seem to be common, there is a vast amount of epigraphical evidence to show that temple charities were not exclusively meant for ceremonials in the temple but also for scientific (śāstraic) and religious (vēdic) education. The South Indian temples served the purposes of educational institutions. Provisions were made for the recitation in temples of hymns from the Dēvāram and other religious poems and for the reading and expounding works of great merit. Adhyāyana (*i. e.* the chanting of the Vēdās) was one of the many objects for which grants were made A large number of records register grants made for the singing of the Tiruppāḍiyam and the Tiruvāymoli hymns. One *inscription records the provision made for the* reading of the Epics like the Mahābhārata and the Rāmāyaṇa and the Purāṇas. One of the Tiruvoṟṟiyūr inscriptions states that as many as 60 vēlis were given for the maintenance of a maṇḍapa built in the temple, for the upkeep of the teachers and pupils who studied grammar in that hall, and for the worship of the god Śivadharma and Siddhānta were also taught[1] In a stone inscription from the Venkatēśa Perumāḷ temple at Tirumukkūdal near Conjeevaram[2] it is stated that besides a hospital, the temple maintained a hostel and a college An epigraph[3] of the time of Rājēndara Chōla I at Eṇṇāyiram (South Arcot District) gives

---

1. A. R. E 1913, p. 110.
2. A R. E. 1916, p. 118 ff.
3. A. R. E. 33 of 1917.

many interesting details to show that temples of South India served the purpose of educational institutions. This inscription is of great importance for it shows clearly that in ancient temples not only was the regular conducting of worship maintained, but also the study of the vēdas, philosophy, grammar and other sciences, and in a few cases, provision was made for a few persons versed in the vēdas. A few of the inscriptions provide grants for the recitation of the Mahābhārata[1], and one of them[2] provides for the recitation of the Bhārata in a maṇḍapa of the temple at Śendalai. A similar endowment occurs in the Kuram plates.[3] Provision seems to have been made now and then for the maintenance of a feeding house *e.g.* provision for feeding 50 students of Śāstras (Copper Plate Grant 5 of 1938).

There are several epigraphs to show the encouragement given to theatres and dances.[4] In the larger South Indian temples, there was invariably a spacious Ranga maṇḍapa. Dancing was practised here and on special occasions dances were staged. The provisions for the amusement of visitors thronging from distant places to witness festivals in temples are occasionally met with in inscriptions. An interesting epigraph[5] records a giftof land to a professional actor for staging themes from Sanskrit Purāṇas. Another epigraph records

---

1. A. R. E. 183 of 1900; 63 of 1897.
2. A R. E 63 of 1897.
3. South Indion Inscriptions, Vol I, p 47
4 A R E 120 of 1925; 152 of 1925, 65 of 1914, 253 of 1914.
5, A. R. E. 120 of 1925.

the provision made for the maintenance of a theatre called Nānāvida-naṭaśālai while two other records[1] register a gift of land for the performance of a dance called Śakki-kuttu and Śāndi-kuttu respectively. The encouragement of music received attention, as for instance, a grant was made Vīṇaikkam for providing music on the Vīṇai in the presence of the god on occasions of worship. An inscription in the Tiṇḍīśvara temple (Tiṇḍivanam) dated in the 10th year (994+1) of the great Chōla King Rājarāja I registers a grant of land for maintenance af a musician who was to play on the lute (Vīṇai).

There are a few instances of a purely literary matter engraved on stone, *e.g.* music inscription at Kudimiyāmalai[2], the Bharatanāṭya verses at Chidambaram[3], the Devāram inscription at Tiruvidavāyil.[4]

The South Indian temple was thus the seat of *free* culture. The temples not only served a social and religious purpose but also were of educational value The reading of the Epics and the recitation of the hymns enabled the people to faithfully follow their religion and enrich their minds. Some of the great classical works in Tamil are said to have been composed in temples.

Closely connected with the temples, there were many Vaishnava and Śaiva mathas which were

1. A. R. E, 65 of 1914, 253 of 1914
2 Epig Indica. Vol XII No 28.
3. A R E 1913-14
4 A R. E 8 of 1918.

both teaching institutions and their educative influence was very great, especially in the Vedas and Śāstras and the Purāṇas The 'mathas,' like the monasteries of mediaval Europe were important religious institutions They were encouraged by the State and possessed a vast amount of wealth There was a religious head for each 'matha' who was highly respected Generally every matha stood for the propagation of a particular school or religion and encouraged teaching and the spreading of knowledge in religious lore Many pious gifts were made to these institutions by the rulers as well as the people and these 'mathas' figured as important adjuncts of the temples for the preservation of traditional culture

A sketch of the main features of the South Indian temple will be incomplete without a reference to their architecture, sculpture and painting The temple architecture reflects the spiritual ideals of the people The South Indian temples are standing monuments of Dravidian architecture The temple craftsman kept alive the traditions of building and metal working embodied in the Śilpaśastras by which all great public works were regulated Speaking of the Dravidian style of architecture Professor Jouveau Dubreuil observes "The Pallava period (600 850) is that of sculptured rocks, the early Chōla period (850-1100) that of grand Vimānas, the later Chōla period *(1100-1350) that of the most beautiful* Gōpuras, the Vijayanagar period (1350-1600) that of Mandapas (pillared halls) and the modern period after 1600 that of corridors "

In brief the great temples of South India were public institutions representing the collective energy of the state rather than monuments for the king's personal glorification. They had civic as well as religious uses; they fulfilled the purposes of a town-hall, college and technical school. The people met in the temple porches to elect representatives for local bodies, to listen to sacred music, recitations or plays. The schools attached to the temple were the repositories of the philosophical lore which were the mainspring of religious life. The records of the religious movements in which the South Indian rulers took an active part have been carefully preserved in both Sanskrit and vernacular literatures, in Śankarāchārya's and Rāmānuja's famous commentaries, in the hymns of Sambandar, Appar and Sundarar and in the Tamil purāṇas. Many temples built by royal command are memorials of them. Images of the Saints and Āḷwārs, who composed hymns in praise of Śiva and Viṣṇu, were set up in temple precincts and the temple structures breathing the spirit of bhakti prove the extraordinary richness of the artistic resources which the rulers commanded. But the temples they built tell nothing of their lives except brief summaries of conquests which made so little impression on the popular memory that whole dynasties were forgotten although their temples are still in daily use.

III

SOURCES

There is abundant evidence in Śaivite literatur to show that Chidambaram is a very sacred plac to followers of Śiva. The sages Vyāgrapāda an Patañjali are said to have been specially blesse there by Śiva in his dance of joy. The temple wa so famous in ancient times that the Dēvāram hymnists simply refer to it as Kōil (*i e* the temple) and it must therefore have existed prior to the ninth century A D. and in some of the inscriptions of the later period, it was generally called Tirukkōyil It was at Chidambaram that the great poet and saint Māṇikkavāśagar is said to have refuted in a contest the Ceylon Buddhists The connection of the temple with the poet-saint Māṇikkavāśagar (if we accept the earlier date for the poet) throws its history still further back: It was in Ponnambalam (*i e* Chidambaram) that the Tamil classics Tiruvāśakam and Periyapurāṇam are said to have been composed Many of the poems of Tiruvāsakam refer specially to 'Chitambalam' or 'Ponnambalam' or 'Hall of Gold', and Māṇikkavāśagar's reference to 'Tillai's Court', where worships all the world, shows that the temple was a great institution even in his time. It was in the temple at Chidambaram that the pariah Saint Nandanār was transfigured into Brahmanhood. Chidambaram is said to be one of the five cities that shared the honour of witnessing the coronations of Chōla Kings Few temples in South India are so rich in epigraphs as the Chidambaram temple Both inscriptions and contemporary literature clearly point to the great antiquity of the temple, and provide interesting and rich material to the student of South Indian history.

The materials for writing the history of the Chidambaram temple are (1) current traditions and legends some of which are interlarded with miracles in the local purāṇas (2) inscriptions and (3) tamil literature The legends of Chidambaram are found in Kōyilpurāṇam which seems to have been written by Umāpati. The legends in this purāṇam relate to a time long antecedent to that of any of the devotees whose stories are given in the Periyapurāṇam and in fact belong to the very oldest period known to South Indian legend. These myths relate specially to Vyāgrapāda, Patañjali, the mystic dance of Śiva and the story of *Hiraṇyavarman, and with these is combined* a great deal of miscellaneous mythology. The Sthala Purāṇas, of which there are many varieties are of no use for historical purposes, but they are interesting in enabling us to understand something of the religious symbolism of the temple.

Almost every temple in South India has an inscription and the largest temples have hundreds of them. Some of them date from the earliest historical times The inscriptions recorded in temples supply us with dates for the several charities made and occasionally for the construction of the temple. But they do not give us any clue as to the origin of the main shrine.

The Chidambaram temple is fortunately rich in epigraphs. The inscriptions of the temple which have been engraved on its walls relate to several

South Indian rulers—Chōla, Pallava, Pāṇdya and Vijayanagar kings—who were the greatest donors to religion. Unfortunately no early epigraphs are found in the temple. As the earlier structures of the temple seem to have undergone renovation, the records so far deciphered do not take us much earlier. Though the antiquity of the temple is attested by archæological evidence as well as by references to early Tamil literature, no contemporary epigraphic material is found in the temple. Again, as the full texts of all the inscriptions have not been published, we have to rely on the summaries of the inscriptions given in the Annual Epigraphical Reports. There is still enough material for scholars to apply their intensive study and draw from the published inscriptions and their texts materials for the reconstruction of South Indian History. The earliests Chōla records in the Chidambaram temple are of those of Rajendra Chōla I dated the 24th year of his reign, and several records of Kulōttunga I, the earliest being the 44th year and the latest the 47th year of his reign. There are several inscriptions of Vikrama Chōla, and of the later Chōlas, notably Kulōttunga III.

The inscriptions of the early Pāṇdyas are not found in the temple, but there are several inscriptions of the mediæval Pāṇdyas—Sundara Pāṇdya I. Vīra Pāṇdya and Vikrama Pāṇdya.

Though the history of the temple goes back, to the Pallava times, no inscriptions relating to early Pallavas are found in the temple. But there are several inscriptions of the great mediæval chieftain, 'Kōpperunjinga' in the Naṭarāja and the Tillai Amman temples in Chidambaram. The inscriptions of the Hindu dynasties of Vijayanagar are found all over South Arcot, and there are a number of epigraphs in the temple relating to the Vijayanagar rulers of the earlier and later dynasties.

Some of the epigraphs of the temple which have their historical introduction give us an insight into the military exploits, the details of administration and the cultural attainment of the times; and they are so far valuable in corroborating the historical achievments of the rulers derived from other sources. Most of the inscriptions which refer to later Chōla kings simply register grants of land for flower-gardens; in some of them gifts of land are made for maintaining worship, offerings, festival in the temple and particularily the special food offering known as 'Pāvādai'. The Chidambaram temple does not seem to possesses many old copper plate grants.[1]

The epigraphical remains of South India are now the only sure source of making out an authentic history of South India, and to scholars interested in South Indian antiquities the South Indian temple is a most interesting institution.

---

1. *Sewell refers to some copper-plate grants. Sewell List of* Antiquities, Vol. 2, p 9. Hultzsch in one of his early Epigraphical Reports says that he saw two copper-plate grants which were dated in Śāka 1621 and 1725 but they do not seem to be of much importance.

Missing Page

6 'Tiruvizha Sargam' describes how Hiraṇyavarman inaugurated the various festivals of the temple (53 stanzas).

The Chidambara Purāṇam of Parañjōti Munivar who lived about A D 1518 belongs to a much later date. The earliest references to Śirrambalam are found in the hymns of the three poet saints—Appar, Sambandar and Sundaramūrthi Devāram or the sacred hymns deserve critical study as genuine works of considerable importance to the students of South Indian history. The evidence furnished by the poet saints may be taken as true, as their writings have come down to us without much change in their reading. The hymns are valuable, as in the case of each hymn one half of each verse describes the god and the other half furnishes a description of the place The religious fervour and ecstasy with which these poets have sung the glories of the temple point to the fact that the Chidambaram temple was regarded as a very sacred institution even long before what is called the Hymnal period in Tamil literature (A D 600-950) Another important work in Tamil literature which deals with the Chidambaram temple is Manikkavaśagar's Tiruvāsagam According to tradition, Tiruvāsagam was sung in the temple itself There are 25 poems dealing exclusively with Tillai. Tiruchchirrambala Kōvai was also composed in Chidambaram by Manikkavāśagar

To the student of South Indian history, Śekkilār's Periyapuranam is of considerable interest and importance The contents of this work, though not the final redaction of it, date from the time before the great Chōla King, Rājarāja I. The Periyapurāṇam which is the history of the sixty-three Śaiva saints mentions the most ancient Śiva temples and it is therefore helpful in determining the antiquity of these temples. This quaint but valuable work was composed during the reign of the Chōla King Anapāya or Kulōttuṅga Cōladēva, but the subject matter of the book is more ancient than the time of the great Rājarāja whose inscriptions record that he set up images of a number of those sixty-three saints in the Tanjore temple which was built by him As regards Śēkkilār's Periyapurāṇam, we can in general depend on its testimony, as the author spared no pains in collecting all the available information of his time, but there is also in it a good deal that is mythological.[1]

1. Periyapurāṇam was composed by Śēkkiḷār who refers to the Cōḷa King by the surname Anapāya The king is said to have been greately attached to the study of Jaina literature and especially the Jīvaka Chintāmani, whose teachings were opposed to the Śaiva faith. Śēkkiḷār undertook to write a complete history of the śaiva saints with a view to converting his master's faith. He proceeded to Chidambaram and prayed to Lord Natarāja for inspiration to perform his assigned task He composed the poem and read it in the Golden Hall—Ponnambalam—before the King and all other devotees The poet was given all royal honours for this great work. The poem consists of 72 cantos in which the lives of 63 saints are given. Probably the ardent Śaivites of the time had felt that they could not retain their hold upon the people without something that should be equivalent to the great canonical books of the Buddhists and the Jains.

The literary references that we find in Tamil literature explain not only the general significance of Śiva's dance but also the details of its concrete symbolism. Of such literature, we may mention Uṇmai Viḷakkam, Tirumūlar's Tirumantaram and Chidambara Mummaṇikōvai. According to Uṇmai Viḷakkam and Tirumūlar's Tirumantaram, the cosmic activity is the central motif of the dance. The dance represents his five activities. The central motive is expanded further in Tirumūlar's Tirumantaram.

" ஆனநட மைந்த கனக களத்த
ஞானநட மாடியைங் கருமத் தாக
வானதொழி லருளாலே தொழிற் செய்தே
தேன்மொழி பாகன் திருநட மாடுமே."

" காளியோ டாடிக் கனகா சலத்தாடிக்
கூளியோ டாடிக் குவலயத் தேயாடி
நீடிய நீர்தீகால் நீள்வா னிடையாடி
நாளுற வம்பலத் தேயாடு நாதனே"

All else but the thought of God must be cast out of the heart that he alone may abide and dance therein. Uṇmai Viḷakkam puts this point clearly.

"மோனந்த மாமுனிவர் மும்மலத்தை மோசித்துத்
தானந்த மானிடத்தே தங்கியிடு—மானந்த
மொண்டருந்தி நின்றாடல் காணுமணு மூர்த்தியாய்க்
கொண்ட திருவம்பலத்தான் கூத்து."

Again the purpose of the dance is stated more explicitly in verses 32, 37 and 39 of Uṇmai Viḷakkam. The supreme intelligence dances in the soul...for the purposes of removing our sins. By these means, our father scatters the darkness

Missing Page

CHAPTER II

THE TRADITIONS OF CHIDAMBARAM

South India is a country where as far back as historical knowledge can reach, one national force has overshadowed all others. It has been the power of a great literary tradition. Political power underwent great changes from time to time under the local rulers, but in the traditions of the people there has been a certain continuity and order. The subject of South Indian tradition and culture is still so unexplored that the best scholar feels least inclined to dogmatise. There is in South India a fine and fascinating literature which, because it has never been studied as early European literatures have been studied, has been ignorantly assumed to be of barbaric interest. In the study of South Indian Culture there is perhaps no study so alluring to the really original mind as this region where scarcely a path is trodden by more than a solitary worker, and where the intelligent worker is sure to find some intellectual reward. The latest researches point to lines of thought which have been too long obscured. No doubt much will be corrected and enlarged in detail, but there are general considerations which cannot be dismissed as having no validity

In some of these traditions, we find a commingling of the traditions of the Áryan and the Dravidian which together form a body of epic material valid for all the peoples old and new. Till comparatively recent times, there have lingered on remnants of oral tradition partly based on historical events, partly the universal folk-lore and partly *mythological* The '*literati*' *of later times* have collected these legends and added to them their own memories. Some of these early traditions seem to work into one framework the histories real or imagined, of the racial elements that make up the present Tamil people. It is in these traditions that we must seek for the soul of the people Religious literature, for instance, has exercised great influence. The number of traditions that has come down to us shows the intensity of the personal religion of the people which could find its appropriate expression only in their native language.

Students of Tamil literature know that in the early history of South India an attempt was made to bring together the great body of religious poems of the Śaiva saints which were till then only preserved in parts at different places. These religious songs had soon acquired the sanctity of the Vēdas among the Tamils. The princes and the people took a keen interest in collecting these hymns. The tradition regarding the rescue of the extant Devāram hymns is told by the Tamil hagiologist Śēkkilar. According to Śekkilār, there lived a great devotee Nambi Āṇdar Nambi during the reign of the Chōla King Rājarāja Abhaya Kulaśēkhara who has been identified with Kuloōttunga I. Nambi was such a great devotee that, according to the story, a dish of rice offered by him was consumed by God. Nambi was credited with miraculous powers and he came to know that the religious hymns sung by the three saints—Jñānaśambandar, Appar and Sundaramūrthi—were preserved on palm leaf in one of the rooms of the Śiva temple at Chidambaram. Finally on opening the room there were found a large number of palm leaf manuscripts of which many had been eaten by moths. The story goes that a voice was heard from above to the effect that the leaves eaten by moths were superfluities Of the three Dēvāram hymnists, Jñānasámbandar is believed to have sung 16,000 hymns but only about 384 of his hymns are now preserved. Similarly some of the hymns of Appar and Sundaramurthi have disappeared. It is generally believed that there were at first many more hymns of these saints than are now available in view of the fact that there were more Śiva temples at that time than are actually found in the hymns.[1]

The Muse of history is nowadays too disdainful of any information that does not reach her signed and counter-signed. In the handling of historical material, it would be a mistake to accept none but documentary evidence, since tradition, if it does not give us truth of fact, at least gives us truth of impression. Ancient Indian tradition is not without its value in the study of local history. The traditionary accounts connected with the origin of dynasties and temples in South India cannot be lightly dismissed as absolutely valueless for historical purposes. There are several instances where traditionary accounts contain some dim historic truth and it therefore becomes the duty of the scientific student who employs higher criticism to disentangle the strands of historic

1. A. R. E. 8 of 1918.

matter from the tangled skein of traditional history. To the student of South Indian temples, in particular, such a sympathetic and critical study of the traditions becomes all the more necessary.

Most of the historic temples of South India are rich in traditions which have deeply coloured the religious and social activities of the people. Some of these traditions are so deeply rooted in the minds of the people that they have been given a prominent social setting Though most of the South Indian temples are of great antiquity, few of them can claim such rich and hoary traditions as the temple at Chidambaram. The history of the temple, so far as can be gathered from historical and archælogical data, may be traced from the early centuries of the Christian era Tradition carries its history still further back and the traditionary account of the origin of the temple is that the sages Vyāghrapāda and Patañjali were engaged in penance at this place in order to get the beatific sight of Śiva's mystic dance ; and pleased with their austerities, Śiva in the form of Naṭarāja with 3,000 Dikshitars known as 'Tillaimūvāyiravar' vouchsafed unto them his Divine Presence. The religious background of the temple is so closely intertwined with some of these traditions that any descriptive account of the temple without these traditions would necessarily be incomplete.

II

Of the various seekers after God whose names are intimately connected with the temple, Vyāgrapāda and Patañjali undoubtedly stand foremost. According to tradition, Vyāgrapāda was the son of an ancient Brahman hermit of North India who dwelt somewhere near the banks of the sacred river Ganges From his early days Vyagrapada became well-versed in the Vedas by sitting at the feet of his father, and he therefore naturally became fired with a desire to learn the highest form of ascetic virtue His father told him that the worship of Śiva was the highest form of virtue he could think of, and so told his son that though Śiva, the supreme Lord exists everywhere, he manifests himself in certain places in this world of which the most famous is the central shrine of Tillai which contains the sacred Ākaśalingam Vyagrapada became anxious to go to that holy place, and after a long journey southwards, reached the forest of Tillai, and took his abode at a place where he saw a tank covered with lotus flowers (Śiva ganga tirtham) and a lingam under the shade of a banyan tree From that day, he dedicated himself to the service of the sacred shrine At the same time, he also chose for himself a permanent abode just a little to the west on the borders of a beautiful tank where he set up a second lingam as his own special shrine and thenceforward divided his services between the sacred spots Vyagrapada soon found that he could not gather flowers from the lofty trees with his frail human body and he therefore prayed to God that he should be endowed with the feet and hands of a tiger armed with strong claws and eyes so that he could climb even lofty trees and see rightly the flowers even in the small hours of the morning His prayer was granted, and so from that time, this fervent devotee of Siva came to be known as Vyagrapada (Tiger-foot) and the place has been called after him as Puliyur (Tiger town)

The story of Patañjali is closely connected with the dance of Śiva. This great devotee was a form of Ādi Śēshan or thousand-headed serpent, on which Viṣṇu slept for ages One day Viṣṇu went to Kailās to worship Śiva who told him that in a neighbouring forest of Tāragam there were a large number of Rishis who were living independent of Śiva's authority. Śiva expressed his intention to visit that forest in order to teach a lesson to those Rishis and Viṣṇu accompaied him. Both Śiva and Viṣṇu entered the forest, Śiva disguised as a mendicant, and Viṣṇu as his wife. At first the Rishis and their wives could not but look at these charming newcomers with a touch of sexual feeling, but they soon recovered from their emotional excitement and found that the mendicant and his wife were not what they seemed They soon raised a sacrificial fire in order to do away with these strangers. A fierce tiger first emerged from the sacrificial fire and rushed upon Śiva who calmly seized it with his hands and tearing off its skin, put it on himself as a mantle. The Rishis still continued their Vedic sacrifices, and then there emerged a serpent which Śiva seized and wreathed round his neck where it ever hangs; and then began His Mystic Dance. Undismayed by these extraordinary acts, the Rishis still continued their prayers, and at last, there appeared a monster in the shape of a blaek dwarf, Muyalagan by name. Śiva now crushed this dwarf by the tip of His sacred foot, thus keeping him writhing underneath his foot and resumed His Mystic Dance which was witnessed by all the gods It may be noted that in every Śiva shrine, the image of Naṭaraja is made to stand on this dwarf The Rishis were now awakened to the splendour of Śiva and became thenceforward his fervent devotees.

After performing the mystic dance, and having taught a lesson to the Rishis, Śiva now went back in triumph to 'Kailas'. Viśnu and Ādiśēshan were overwhelmed by the mystic dance of Śiva and Ādhiśeshan was seized with a desire to behold the dance once again Viśnu accordingly released Ādiśeshan from further service, and exhorted him to go to 'Kailās' to obtain the beatific vision by a life of asceticism So Ādiśeshan went to 'Kailās' and devoted himself to penance and meditation. At last Śiva appered in the form of Brahma, riding upon a swan, and pleased with the austerities of Ādiseshan offered him any boon he desired Ādiśēshan replied that he desired to see the mystic dance of the God of gods At last Śiva revealed himself to the great Yōgi who became thenceforth his true disciple, and promised to show him the mystic dance in sacred Tillai which is the exact centre of the universe Ādiśeshan was therefore bidden to go to that sacred place, but as the inhabitants of the earth would take fright on account of his form, he transformed himself into a man retaining in part his serpent form Accordingly Ādiśeshan who had now become part man and part serpent under the name of Patañjali went to the forest of Tillai where he met Vyāgrapāda and made for himself a hermitage and a 'lingam' to perform his daily worship

The earliest account of these traditions is to be found in Chidambara Mahātmya, originally found in palm leaves and written in grantha characters. *The purport of this manuscript is noticed in* the Mackenzie Collection as follows :—

"Legend of the celebrated temple of Chidambarēśvara reputed site of the hermitage of Vyāgrapāda,[1] an inspired grammarian, and of Patañjali, *an incarnation of the serpent,* Sēsha and first teacher of the Yōga; in latter times, it is celebrated as the final residence of Māṇika Vāśagar and other characters of note in the traditions of the south; the legend is said to belong to the Skanda Purāṇas.[2]"

A full account of these two great devotees of Śiva is given in the Kōyil Purāṇam written by Umāpathi a great Śaiva Schoolman, and belongs to the earliest period of South Indian tradition and they may be taken to refer to the earliest period of the establishment of the Brahmanical system in South India. The name Vyāgrapāda is mentioned in the Rig Vēda and the story of Vyāgrapāda is anterior to that of Patañjali. The story of the struggle between Śiva and the Rishis may be taken to refer to some early conflict between the Vēdāntists and the Śaivities. The Rishis may be the adherents of the Pūrva

---

1. The following stanza in Kolpuranam refers to the 'mūla-sthāna' in Tillai as the place of worship of Vyāgrapāda

"ஞாலத்தார் பிரகோடி கற்றுன முனைவற்றி
னேலத்தா லவமார விடைகொண்ட வெழிற்றில்லை
மூலத்தா னத்தோனியாய முளைத்தெழுந்த சிவலிங்க
கோலத்தா னினைபூசை கொள்வான."

—(Kōyilpurāṇam, Vyāgrapāda Sargam)

2 Mackenzie Collection, Vol I, p. 71

Mīmāmsa school founded by Jaimini. It was to convince them of the limited power of their orthodox sacrifices that Śiva appeared as the 'Bhikshatana Murti' (mendicant deity) The symbolism of the other parts of the story is sought to be explained in this way Śiva subdues and wraps round him the tiger-like fury of human passion The malice of mankind in the form of a serpent is worn by Śiva as his necklace, and the black dwarf writhing under the tip of his toe is the monster of a human depravity. Śiva is represented in these stories, sometimes as gracious and sometimes as malignant, and the composite character of the Śaiva religion in South India may be due to the influence of the cult of the pre-Aryan races in South India The story of the dance at Tillai 'enshrines the record of an ancient rivalry between the priests of the Aryan deities and the devotees of Dravidian gods The coming down of Śiva to his famous shrine at Tillai in order to perform the mystic dance for the beatification of his two great devotees Vyāghrapāda and Patañjali is associated with a most interesting legend According to the story, in Chidambaram, then known as Tillai, there were at first two shrines—one to Śiva and another to goddess Kali just where the Nritta Sabha now stands When Śiva came down to Tillai to perform the dance, Kali, the local presiding deity of the place, would not allow him to enter her domain Finally they they agreed to settle their superiority by the dance, and whichever of them danced better should become master of the place and the vanquished should go out of the place

Then began the great Dance in the midst of devotees at the place, where the Nritta Sabha now stands. After a fairly equal contest for a long time, Śiva resorted to his famous dance by raising one of his legs above his head—a dance which was impossible for Kāḷi. The goddess Kāḷi had therefore to own her discomfiture and leave the place choosing for herself an abode outside the precincts of Tillai, The temple of Kāḷi or Tillai Amman Koil, as it is popularly called, is now on the outskirts of Chidambaram as evidence of the old saying Tillaikkāḷi ellaikkappâlē (தில்லைக்காளி எல்லைக்கப்பாலே). This famous dance of Śiva is commemorated in the Nritta Sabha by one of the finest dancing icons of Nataraja.

According to tradition, the temple which was of divine origin was repaired and enlarged by Simhavarman in the 6th century A. D. as a mark of his piety and gratitude for the cure of his leprosy by a bath in the Sivaganga tank, and this king came to be known after this miracle as Hiraṇyavarman (the golden armoured).

The Hiraṇyavarman tradition is one of great importance to the student of the Chidambaram temple. The history of the Tamil country is, as gathered from early inscription, goes to show that the Pallavas were supreme in South India We have Simhavarman II mentioned in the Uṛuvapalli plates. The initial date of Simhavarman II is said to be the middle of the 5th century and he is said to have ruled about 20 years. Little is known from copper plates and inscriptions about

Simhavarman III who occupied the Pallava throne before Simhavarman began to rule at Kānchi about the last quarter of the 6th century A D

The traditionary account of Simhavarman is found in *Koilpuranam* written by Umapathi (who lived early in the 14th century) and also in Chidambara Mahātmyam According to tradition Simhavarman and his two brothers Vedavarman and Sumati were descended from Manu—Simhavarman by the first wife, and the other two by the second wife Simhavarman was of a highly religious turn of mind from his early days and wanted to get away from the burdens of royalty as he was stricken with leprosy and started to go on a pilgrimage to all Saiva shrines He visited the Vanga country and the country of Bhīsmēśwara who had the 'Rishaba' standard and then came to the Andhra country where he visited Kalahasti In his travels in the South, he came upon a hunter and asked him to narrate something about his adventures in the southern forests Fired with a desire to see the places described by the hunter, he began roaming through the forests and finally reached the forest of Tillai where he saw Vyāghrapāda doing penance He bathed in the Sivaganga tank and was immediately cured of his leprosy so that he came to be known thereafter as Hiranyavarman Out of gratitude for the cure of this lifelong disease, he built the several structures of the temple Thereupon Vyaghrapāda blessed Hiranyavarman with the duty of guarding Vyāghrapura *i e* Tillai by giving him the flag with the tiger crest.[1] Koilpurāṇam (stanza II, Tiruvizha sargam) describes Hiraṇyavarman as the prince who wore the 'Atti' (அத்திப்பூ) garland. In stanza 12 of Koilpuraṇam, Hiraṇyavarman is referred to as the Chōḷa prince. The whole of the modern South Arcot formed a part of the ancient Toṇdaimaṇdalam. The history of Toṇdaimaṇdalam from the middle of the 4th century A. D. to the succession to the throne of Simhaviśhṇu 575 A. D. is obscured by the activities of Kalabhras one of whose rulers Achyuta is said to have had his capital at Chidambaram. From the time of Simhaviśhṇu (675—600 A. D.) to the time of Paramēśhvara Varman II the order of succession of Pallava kings presents but little difficulty. The whole country comprised by South Arcot came under the rule of the Pallavas in the time of Simhaviśhṇu After Paramēsvara Varman II came Nandivarman Pallavamalla (710-775 A. D.) the son of Hiraṇyavarman being sixth in descent from Bhīmavarman, the younger brother of Simhaviśhṇu. The Chidambara Mahātmyam ascribes the enlargement of the temple to Simhavarman who being cured of his disease became known as Hiraṇyavarman. Hiraṇyavarman was the father of Nandivarman Pallavamalla and the temple, if the identification is correct, must have been built in the 8th century A. D. But the temple is mentioned in Dēvāram which takes us to the 7th century and earlier periods. Temples though not of stone structures

1. "புத்தி யிலக்கு புலிப்பதி காவல் புரப்பாவென
நற்றமிழ் முந்து பணிக்கொடி யக்கை பாத்திரப்த்து."
(Koilpurāṇam)

must have existed in the pre Pallava period as can be seen from the evidence of Sangam literature The earliest structure of the temple—the Chit sabha, a shrine built of wood—points to its earlier existence and the temple might have assumed a new form in the last century of Pallava rule and very much enlarged during the time of the mediaeval Chōlas

III

Among the numerous South Indian Saints, there are few that have been invested with the halo of such a rich and beautiful legend as Nanda, the Pariah Saint Nanda was born in the village of Ādanur He was a Pariah by caste-a caste which has been regarded as being outside the pale of the important Hindu castes From his early days, Nanda was remarkably devout The small circular Gōpura or tower of the Śiva temple in the Brahman surroundings of Ādanur had a strange fascination for his boyish imagination It is said that, as the village god passed in procession during festivals, Nanda would run up to obtain a view, however distant, of the God and return deeply impressed with the procession and its poetic association

As he grew to manhood his imaginative fervour and piety also deepened and he became anxious to *do what he could for the service of the Lord* The course of true love never runs smooth, and Nanda had been yearning to see what specific services could be rendered by a poor man like him to please the Lord The fact that his low birth stood in the way of rendering divine service began to torment him At last, one day while thinking seriously over the matter, the idea dawned on him that he might supply temples with leather for drums. He was so much taken up by this sudden thought that he henceforth began to devote himself ardently to procuring and tanning leather as a sacred pastime and singing in praise of god day in and day out.

One day while there was no work to be done in the fields he stole a march with a few friends to the *neighbouring famous temple of* Tirupūṅgūr (now known as old Vaithīswaran Koil.) Nanda was beside himself with joy when he saw for the first time from a distance the sanctum sanctorum of the great temple. Tradition asserts that as Nanda was standing behind the flagstaff and struggling to get a view of the 'Liṅgam' inside, Śiva took pity on him and ordered Nandi (the image of a bull placed opposite to the Liṅgam in all Śaivite temples) to move a little to one side so that his low-caste devotee might get a glimpse of Him; and to this day, the huge figure of Nandi at Tirupūṅgūr is placed not exactly opposite to the image of Śiva but a little leaning to one side.

The story goes that after his first devotional trance, Nanda soon came to know the glories of Chidambaram as the holiest place and that he who once visits that temple crosses once and for ever the ocean of birth and death. From that day onward, Chidambaram exercised a strange mystery over him Nanda became fired with a desire to visit the great temple Whether he worked in the fields or stayed at home, or went to sleep, he had always in his mind the great God dancing as it were the unceasing dance of creation, destruction and maintenance. Nanda's repeated and passionate mutterings to his friends that he would visit Chidambaram the next day earned for him the nickname 'Tirunāḷaippōvār' (one that goes to-morrow.)

when they are taken literally, seem to have a meaning. As Renan, the French critic observes, 'faith demands the impossible, nothing less will satisfy it'. To this very day the Hindus every year walk over glowing coals in order to attest the virginity of Draupadi, the common wife of the five sons of Kunti..........a narrative anecdotal and fabulous in form may be more true than the truth itself; the glory of a legend belongs in a sense to the great man whose life that legend traces, and who has been able to inspire in his humble admirers qualities which apart from him, they could never have invented. Often the hero creates his own legend.

Some modern pandits have endeavoured to explain what they consider as the philosophic truth under-lying the Nandan legend. Nanda is none but 'Ātman' *i.e.* Ānanda or bliss which is god. In the words of Taittariya Upaniṣhad, "He recognised that Happiness is Brahman; from Happiness, indeed, all these creatures are born; when born, they live through Happiness; when they depart, they enter into Happiness."[1] Nanda's nativity in a 'Parachēri' is taken to signify that we are dealing in flesh and blood The very thought we bestow on our body is a 'parishad', so to say and requires a 'Prayaschittam' (purification). The Parachēri which is generally remote from the temples represents Avidya or ignorance. The temple which is always visible at a distance signifies the hope that animates man. Nandi (Śiva's bull) which

1. Taittariya Upanishad, III-6.

obstructs the view signifies the four good tendencies of the mind, cheerfulness, calmness, patience and resignation, and it is through these qualities that God is approached. Nanda goes to Chidambaram to the presence of the 'Ātman' and he may be said to have reached the stage when he could find, 'tongues in trees, books in the running brooks, sermons in stones and good in everything.' The Dikshitars are the 'Sastraic' support and love required for entering Divine Presence. Nanda passes through the ordeal of fire—the pitfalls through which one has to pass in life; when he emerges from the fire and is led into the temple, he enters into the Divine Presence which the ordinary little minds cannot see. In fact Nanda's story is an illustration of the great teaching; "whosoever will save his life, shall lose it; and whosoever will lose his life for my sake shall find it.'

Apart from the traditions, the most interesting and important question for us is the question of the historicity of Nandan or Nandanār, as he is commonly called Nandan's name is first mentioned as 'Tirunāḻaippōvār' in one of the poems of Sundaramūrti. Nandanār is one of the 63 Saivite saints whose praises are being sung in Periyapurāṇam by Śekkilār who flourished in the first half of the 12th century. But the story of Nandanar became popular only by the musical compositions (Kīrtanas) of Gopalakrishna Bharati of Anataṇḍavapuram. This work is commonly known as Nandanār Sarittaıa Kīrtanạ. It seems that Bharati has deviated from the original of Periyapurāṇam by introducing into the story a

Missing

Page

825 A.D. There is no shadow of doubt that to Sundaramūrti, 'Nāḷaipōvār' (நாளைப்போவார்) was a historical figure. How long before Sundaramūrti did he live? Who were his contemporaries? These are questions to which no answer can be given in the present state of our knowledge. But the name Nandan does not occur in Sundaramūrti's Tevaram. He is simply called 'Nāḷaipōvār' (நாளைப் போவார்) That the Periyapurāṇam is not strictly historical in all its details one need not say. Certainly there are a few myths around the person of Nandan. The Periyapurāṇam story of Nandan contains much that is legendary. But we are safe in saying that it is a legend or group of legends round a historical being Nandan who became one of the most revered Saivite saints as early as the 9th century A.D.

IV

MĀṆIKKAVĀŚAGAR LEGEND

Another famous saint who is said to have attained his salvation in Chidambaram is Māṇikkavāśagar. His later life is closely associated with the Chidambaram temple His history is very much obscure but we can infer from the legends connected with his name that he was a remarkable Saiva devotee who played no small part in recovering South India from the Buddhists and the Jains. His date is still controversial and ranges from the 3rd to the 12th century A.D. Evidently he lived at a time when the influence of Buddhism in South India was declining. It is now generally believed that he lived about the 9th century of our era. We are not concerned here with the early history of Māṇikkavāśagar. The scene of his greatest achievements was Chidambaram. In later days he devoted his whole time to the glorification of Tillai. Many of his hymns in Tiruvāchakam in reference to the god in Tillai are beautiful. The Tiruvāchakam is said to have *been composed by the saint at Tillai by divine* interposition.

There was much intercourse between Ceylon and South India in those days and the King of Ceylon with his court arrived at Chidambaram with his dumb daughter with the intention of overthrowing the citadel of Saivism—the God of Ponnambalam. The three thousand devotees of the temple who were now in a fix were asked by God himself to send for Māṇikkavāśagar. Thus bidden by God the sage came from his place of meditation at Pichavaram and entered into a disputation with the Buddhists. The details of the disputation are set forth in Tiruvātavūrar Purāṇam. At the close of the discussion, the saint made his appeal to Sarasvathi who made the Ceylon heretics dumb. Thereafter the Ceylon king became a convert as also his dumb daughter who now got gift of speech and she herself refuted the absurdities of the Buddhist gurus. The substance of her words is supposed to be given in the Charal song (Tiruvāchakam—திருச்சாழல்). When Māṇikkavāśagar was asked to give an authoritative exposition of the meaning of the whole, he proceeded to the Golden Hall and pointed to the image of God adding, The Lord of the Assembly himself (Sabhapathi) is the meaning and Māṇikkavāśagar then disappeared melting into the image of his Master.

Māṇikkavāśagar's hymns connected with his victory are even now sung in the temple on the anniversary of the event. From this poetical legend it is difficult to sift any history. It would seem as if there was in this legend a vague reminiscence of some great expedition of the king of Ceylon with the double intention of conquering the country and of establishing Buddhism. As regards these legends, some are inclined to treat them as wonderful stories and nothing more. There are others who believe these legends devoutly and regard them as capable of some mystic interpretation and yet there are some who think under the veil of such legends ancient sages conceded mysterious teachings which they were unwilling to expose to the vulgar gaze. The mystic interpretations are to be found in later and especially South Indian authors The Saiva Siddhanta philosophers tried to give the legends a more elevating interpretation and this is possibly due to the fact that the south of India has from the earliest times been more open than the rest of the country to western influences and teaching.

V

INSTITUTIONAL ASPECTS OF THE TEMPLE

One of the most interesting and unique features of the Chidambaram temple is its administration by a group of Brahman priests known as Dīkṣhitars. According to traditionary accounts the pagoda arose when the Lord Nataraja together with 3,000 Dīkṣhitars appeared at this place to bless his great devotees, Vyāghrapāda and Patañjali. The Dīkṣhitars claim themselves to be of divine origin and according to them, Brahma took them from Tillai to perform a 'Yāgam' near Benares where they stayed till Hiraṇyavarman at the suggestion of the Chidambaram deity invited them back to Chidambaram. When they had arrived they found that there were only 2,999 and a voice from above announced that the God himself, Sabha Nayakar, was the missing one. These traditions seem to imply that from the inception of the temple the Dīkṣhitars have been regarded as a part aud parcel of the institution. Tamil literature tends to confirm the antiquity of the Dīkṣhitars. The earliest literary reference to the Dīkṣhitars are to be found in Dēvāram. In Dēvāram, the sacred books of the Saivites, one of the poet-saints says. "I am the servant and devotee of Tillai Mōōvāyiravar." Sundaramūrti, in his Tiruttoṇdatokai, gives a list of the famous saints. Besides the names of the saints, the list gives the names of nine companies of saints called Tolkai Adiyārkal to make room for all else who might have attained salvation. Of these, he mentions Tillaivazh Andaṇar (lit, the Brahmins living at Chidambaram but really the 3000 Brahmins) attached to the shrine as evident from interpretation of Sēkkilār.[1] Sambandar, one

1. See தில்லை வாழ்ந்தணர் புராணம் in Periyapurāṇam.

of the Dēvāram hymnists in one of his hymns describes the Tillaivāzh Andaṇar as he actually saw them.[1]

Nambi Āṇdār Nambi refers to the Tillaivāzh Andaṇar in his "Tirutoṇḍatiruvantāti" in the following quotation :—

"செப்பத் தகுப்புகழ்தில்லைப் பதியிற் செழுமறையோ
ரொப்பப் புவனங்கள் மூன்றினுமும் பரினூரெரித்த
வப்பர்க் கமுதத்திருநடர்க்கந்திப் பிறையணிந்த
துப்பர்க் குரிமைத்தொழில் புரிவோர்தமைச்
சொல்லுவதுமே,"

Sēkkizhar's description of the Tillaivāzh Andaṇar in Periyapurāṇam makes it appear that the Dīkṣhitars were well versed in the Śāstras and were animated by no other purpose than that of devotion and service to Naṭarāja These references in Tamil Literature show very clearly that the Dīkshitars have been intimately associated with the Temple even before the hymnal period. The great esteem in which the Dīkshitars of the temple were held by the princes and the people may be seen from the account in Periyapurāṇam The purāṇam for instance refers to the fact that a petty chieftain of Kalandār who was celebrated later as Kurrva Nāyaṉar wanted the Brahmans of Chidambaram (apparently the Tillai Mūvāiravar) to invest him with the diadem and thus confer

---

1. "நீலத்தார் கரிய மிடற்றார் நல்ல
நெற்றிமே லுற்ற கண்ணினார் பற்று
சூலத்தார் சுடலைப்பொடி நீறணிவார் சடையார்
சீலத்தார் தொழுதேத்து சிற்றம் பலம்."

—Dēvāram

the dignity of royalty on him in recognition of his extensive conquests, but the Brahmans declined on the ground that only the ancient family of the Chōlas was entitled to this high privilege.

At present the number of Dīkṣhitars has dwindled; and there are are now about 250 married members. They are an endogamous clan. They never live outside Chidambaram and they are enjoined not to resort to any other occupation or means of livelihood than that of service and devotion to Nataraja. The Dīkṣhitars have been the hereditary trustees of the temple; and the management of the temple and its affairs have been vested entirely in their hands.

Every Dīkṣhitar as soon as he is married, becomes as of right a trustee and 'archaka' of the temple, and his trusteeship is inalienable. The trusteeship does not descend from father to son, but it inheres in every member of the community of the Dikshitars at Chidambaram from his birth so that in a particular family there may be at the same time both father and sons having an equal voice in the management of the institution. In no other temple does a whole community form the trustees and 'archakas' at one and the same time with every member of the community having rights of management from his birth The Dīkshitars are a democratic joint-family group for religious purposes, the Lord Naṭarāja being the family 'Deity' and 'Upāsanamūrti' of every Dīkṣhitar. The worship in the temple is conducted in what is known as 'Vaidik pooja' and this temple is the one solitary instance in which this 'Vaidik pooja' which resembles in its ritual that of domestic worship, is followed, while the 'pūja' in other temples in South India is of the Āgama form.

This temple has had, unlike all other South Indian temples, no landed property. The temple has not received at any time, and does not receive any 'Mōhini' or 'Tāsdik' allowance from Government. No accounts are kept. Though inscriptions afford instances of permanent grants of property or other endowments in the name of the deity by Hindu kings, there is at present no property in the name of the temple. It can only be explained by the fact that the temple has been allowed to be entirely dealt with and managed by the Dīkshitars themselves, as if it were their own property. A Dīkshitar is entitled to perform 'pūjas' and 'archanas' only after he is initiated in the 'pūja'.

The temple worship has been conducted partly by contributions by the Dīkshitars themselves from their own funds and by the collection of subscriptions from their constituents and, in the major part, by the periodical benefactions of the numerous devotees. There are six daily 'pūjas' which are met out of the 'kaṭṭaḷais' established by pious and charitable devotees. The help given by the people by means of money for conducting the necessary affairs of the temple is called 'kaṭṭaḷai.' That these 'kaṭṭalais' have been instituted from early times is borne out by some inscriptions. For instance, an inscription[1] on the south gōpura of the temple (right entrance) and another inscription[2]

1. A. R. E. 349 of 1913.
2. A. R. E. 362 of 1913.

in the west gōpura of the temple (right entrance) both dated Śāka 1510, record that provision made by Vaiyappa Kṛishnappa Koṇḍama-Nāyaka for 20 offerings to be distributed among Śaiva mendicants (paradēśi) in the temple was placed under the supervision of Nāmaśivāya Udaiyār, 'the superintendent of all services' (kaṭṭalai). The Dīkṣhitars have nothing to do with these 'kaṭṭalais'. The agents of the 'Kaṭṭalidars' give the articles necessary for the daily 'pūja' in kind at the time of the 'pūjas' and the accounts are kept by them. The Dīkṣhitars are not entitled to ask for the accounts. For 'kāla pūja' there are on an average about six such 'kaṭṭalais' and each of them contributes a small portion of the articles necessary for the 'pūja'. The value of such daily contributions may vary from half a rupee to three rupees at the highest.

The numerous festivals celebrated in the temple may be classified as follows:-(*a*) The monthly or 'Panchaparva' festivals; (*b*) other festivals during the year; and (*c*) the two 'Brahmōthsavams' in the months of December and June.[1] These festivals are also celebrated from out of the contributions of various 'Ubayakārs'. As regards the two 'Brahmōthsavams' which last for ten days, entire castes such as Kaikōlars, Veḷḷālars, Oil-mongers etc. perform the festivals on particular days in the ten days from out of the subscriptions

1. Pachaiyappa, the great educational benefactor, with the assistance of Manali Chinniah Mudaliar, inaugurated the June festival on June 28, 1791. He had the Car of the God renovated at the time.

which they levy from the members of their own caste. The expenses for other annual festivals and the 'panchaparva' festivals are incurred by individual 'Ubayakārs'. In many cases, the individual 'Ubayakārs' change from year to year.

The only source of income is that derived from the general offerings in the temple and such offerings are, from immemorial usage, the property of all the trustees and constitute the recognised mode of livelihood of the Dīkshitars. This immemorial usage has been recognised by Muthuswami Ayyar and Sheppered, J.J, as follows:—" About 250 families of Dīkṣhitars reside at Chidambaram and the net income of the temple which is derived from the general offerings is their recognised means of livelihood According to usage, every Dīkṣhitar is entitled on marriage to take part in the management, to do 'pūja' or perform service in the minor shrines, and to share in the emoluments of the institution."

These offerings are divided among the Dīkshitars in the temple. The right of collecting these offerings is given to a batch of 20 Dīkṣhitars who are on duty in the pagoda for 20 days at a time, and they have the charge of the keys of the respective shrines within the temple known as the Five kōils and the custody of the jewels and other valuable articles in those shrines which are examined once in four days, and they guard the temple during nights In this manner the right goes round to all the trustees during the year The key to the common treasury room is with 20 persons who are the 'turn' men The daily incomes of the temple go to the 'turn' people. If there is a lessee, they will go to him; if not, they will go to the 'turn' men.

The temple servants were originally paid in kind out of the offerings of the temple, but now they are supplemented by small cash payments from the common fund. The ancient and undisputed rule of the temple is that all the Dīkṣhitars manage its affairs in common and that the 'vētō' of any one of them is sufficient to prevent the execution of the business. The 'common man' goes to every house and gives verbal information that a meeting will take place. The meetings are conducted in a particular portion of the temple. The system of management of the temple is peculiar and unique. Every Dīkṣhitar has a vote and voice in the management of the temple, and they together form a truly democratic body. All personal relations and private differences are set aside when the Dīkṣhitars meet in a body to discuss the affairs relating to the temple All questions affecting the management of the temple are decided at the periodical meetings of the community by the vote of the majority, and the resolutions of the community are recorded in regular books maintained for the purpose. There are elaborate rules and improvised checks for preventing mismanagement and misappropriation, and these rules are strictly followed in the conduct and procedure of their meetings, and in the actual management of temple affairs; and the delinquents are fined or suspended by resolutions passed by the Dīkṣhitars at their meetings. Rules have been framed for the purpose of checking the various items of jewellery in the temple and for the purpose of guarding the temple during nights by the Dīkshitars themselves Particular members are made responsible for the proper conduct of festivals and other services in the temple by the system of leasing out the right to collect the offerings on these occasions to a few individuals among them at the assembly of the Dīkshitars, and making them accountable to the the whole body of Dīkshitars for the successful conduct of these festivals and services.

The jewels of the temple contain some which are presents made by various Rājāhs. There are lists in the respective temples, giving particulars of the names of the Rājāhs, the jewels they presented and the places where they are kept Among them there is a jewel called 'Nalan Patakkam'. The jewels are kept safely in a box in the respective temples and the keys of the boxes are in the custody of some Dīkshitars deputed for the purpose The person having the keys must hand them over the next day to the person taking charge.

CHAPTER III

DESCRIPTION OF THE TEMPLE

The Śiva temples in South India are generally longer from East to West, but the temple at Chidambaram is longer from south to north The temple covers an area of about 40 acres The main edifices of the temple are enclosed with two high walls of dressed granite and they constitute the fourth prakāra of the temple and consist of extensive garden lands with flower gardens belonging to the temple Outside these high walls run the four car streets about 60 ft. in width which are said to cover the site formerly occupied by the ditch which once formed part of the fortifications. Through both the high walls run the four main gateways or entrances to the temple The four main entrances at the inner high wall are surmounted by towers or gōpuras.

The temple within the outer high walls covers a great open space of 300 yards in length and 250 yards in width, paved with stone slabs and this constitutes the third prakara of the temple, and in the enclosure the most important edifices are the Amman shrine, the Pāṇdiyanayaka or Subrahmaṇya shrine, the Sivaganga tank and on either side of this tank are the 100 pillared maṇdapa and the 1000 pillard maṇdapa and the shrine of Gaṇapathi midway between the southern and western gōpuras. The innermost enclosures of the temple are the most ancient and sacred portion of the temple and special sanctity attaches to the five halls or sabhās—the Chit sabhā, the Kanaka sabhā, the Nritta sabha, the Dēva sabha and the Rāja sabhā.

The Chit sabhā which is the central shrine is the most sacred and ancient portion of the temple. *Śiva is worshipped here in the form of Naṭarāja* and the Chit sabhā contains the sacred chamber called Rahasya where there is no image or 'liṅgam' but a string of 'vilva' leaves and the explanation is that it is the abode of Śiva in his ākāśa or ethereal form There is Thiruvâśi (a semi-circular figure) in the wall over that the screen hangs The 'Rahasya' is within the circumference of the Thiruvâśi on the wall The temple itself is not named after the deity who so manifested himself in that shape; probably he was incomprehensible in that form, but in commemoration of a later manifestation of Iśvara in the form of Natarâja which literally means 'Lord of Dancing'. The steps leading to the sabha are five in number and represent the five letters of the holy mantra, Pançhâkshara and every portion of the sabha including nails, tiles, pillars etc,, is said to have a holy significance The following extracts from the Ŝtalapurânas explain the symbolism of the Chit sabha: Chidambara Mahatmyam —

Cânto 15:—There is a sabha called Ambara which is the abode of all good In it I constantly dance in happiness. It is Chidambaram and consequently it is revered by all

Cânto 18 —As I who am pure occupy the soul which is in the body, even so in the world which is (like) the body I sport in Chidambaram

Cânto 85 —This called Chidambaram is (my) body, and I am the free soul

(Pundarikapura Mahâtmyam Canto 59) —That sabha (hall) is of the nature of chit (Divine knowledge) and there is no doubt it is of the nature of chit.

(Thillaivana Mahâtmyam Canto 63):—The Chit Sabha which is in the middle of Virât Purusha (the great spirit) is an old one

Mahāmāya is in the middle, facing the south. In the western wall, pure Thirōdāna is said to reside. But in the eastern part there is the independent Māya in the shape of a wall. It (the wall) is the cause of the creation and absorption of the nine Tattavas beginning with Brahma. The screen is said to be Thirōdha Sakti having the shape of Prasāda.

... ...

Of the length of 96 angulas of the same breadth

... ...

The Vēdhi of Darsana shines on the southern part. The Yantram of that name is small, invisible and imperceptible.

... ...

It is the mine of Kāmadhēnu and it is the abode of Sankha and other Nidhis. It is well worshipped by Svarna Karshana Bhairava and the eight Lakshmis.

On its left side is placed the excellent Sparsana Chakra.

... ...

The Vēdas, Rig, Yaju, Sāma and Atharvana; the Purāṇas, Agamas the Arts, the Mechanical Arts, Sacred Knowledge, etc., accordingly went soon to Pundarikapuram. The 64 Kalas and Vidyas (branches of knowledge) have on earth changed (their shape) as Vidyas.

... .

They separately took their abode in the several places in the shape of pillars, mountains beams, windows, wood, nails, gold plates, silver, copper stone and earth.

... ...

In the South east is Rig (Vēda); the Siraś or head is in the middle. These two are said to be pillars. There are two (others) on the west.

... ...

These reside in Sadāsiva Pītha over it. But in Iswara Pitha there are shastras numbering as many as there are karmas *i. e.* (six). These with the Angas exist in the shape of pillars under sada.

... ...

The pillars consisting of (representing) the five elements are in *Rudra's* Vēdi.

... ...

In the middle of Vishnu's Vedi there are various kinds of Tattvas. The Tattvas are in the shape of windows according to different sorts.

... ...

The group of 96 Tattavas is clearly here in the shape of windows in five rows. In their midst the Agamas have come in the shape of pillars. The great Goddess of Divine Knowledge consisting of Chit has taken visible form and this incomparable salvation has taken its abode in the southern doorway.

... ...

On the upper part of the ceiling of the Sabha all the 64 Kalas (Arts) taking the shape of beams exist separately.

... ...

The various worlds numbering 224 are in the shape of planks. The inspirations and expirations numbering 21,600 are like gold leaf.

... ...

All the various kinds of nerves numbering 72,000 having taken the shape of rails.

... ...

The Saktis, Vāma, Gyestha, Rowdri, Kāḷi, Kāḷivikariṇi, Bāli, Bālavikariṇi, Pramathani, Manōnmaṇi, these exist in the shape of stupis (domes).

There are nine kalasams placed over the Chit Sabha These kalasams are placed in a row. The Panchakshara steps leading to the Chit Sabha are stone steps plated with silver for adorning them.

The Chit Sabha is built with four corners, the length being greater from east to west, and shorter from south to north. On the three sides of the Sabha there are wooden walls on the stone basement and on the 4th side there are wooden doors, windows and pillars. The beams are placed over five pillars.

The Kanaka Sabha is in front of the Chit Sabha and forms part of it. It is here that all the daily rituals to the god in Chit Sabha are performed.

The Nritta Sabha or 'Hall of the Dance' is one of the oldest edifices of the temple and is associated with an interesting legend of the Dance of Śiva as Natarāja and the Dance has given its name to the Sabha. The Nritta Sabha is a little to the south of the Kanaka Sabha.

The Dēva Sabha which is a little to the east of the Chit Sabha and which lies in the second prakara of the temple is another shrine where the Dikshitars now hold their Committee meetings connected with the affairs of the temple.

The Chit Sabha and the Kanaka Sabha are enclosed by a wall which separates it from the Mūlasthāna and this wall which bears some of the earliest records of Vikrama Chōla dated 3rd year of of his reign is known in four inscriptions as Kulotunga Śōlan tirumāligai and Vikrama-śōlan tirumāligai in three others. The first prakāra of the temple thus surrounding the central shrine of Natarāja might have been the work of Vikrama Chōla the son and successor of Kulōttunga I The second prakāra wall which encloses the Mūlasthāṉa shrine is also called Vikrama Śōlan tirumāligai [1]

The Mūlasthāna shrine which according to tradition was the most ancient shrine round which all other shrines have been built is the most important edifice in the second enclosure and there are two mandapas in the second enclosure, one on the northern and one on the southern side From one of the inscriptions[2] it can be inferred that the Mūlasthāṉa shrine was known as 'Edirambalam.'

The shrine of Vishnu is in the first enclosure of the temple close by the Chit Śabha and the Kanakasabha The Vishnu shrine possesses a Balipīta, a flagstaff and a Garuda shrine It has a

---

1 A R E 290 of 1913

The following stanza in Koyilpurānam by Umapathi Sivāchārya refers to the fact that the Chit Śabha is to the south of the Mūlasthana shrine of the temple

"நாட்டு நடுவிலொடி நலங்கிளர் தில்லை நேர்போயக
கூடு மகத்தினில் மூலக்குறியுள தக்குத் தென்னர்
மாடுறு மறைகள் காணு மன்று மம்பலமென்றுண்டம
காடுது மென்று மென்று மென்னை யாளுடையவன

2 A R E 290 of 1913

small prakāra. Close by is the shrine of the Viṣṇu Goddess. These paraphernalia are not found in most other Vishṇu shrines said to exist in Śiva temples and may be taken to indicate that Viṣṇu is not a subordinate deity in this temple. According to Puṇḍaīkapura Mahātmya, Viṣṇu had come to protect the place in the form of Gōvindarāja.

Though the main shrine is a small structure which has attained to great sanctity, the court-yards, gopuras and other exterior structures have been added to it by succeeding kings in such a manner that the original small central shrine cannot be seen from outside.

The four great gōpuras of the temple have been built by some of the kings at different periods. The four gōpuras are visible even from the sea and it is said that the gōpuras and the lights which are lit on them on holy days have served as well-known landmarks for mariners. That the northern gōpura was built by Krishṇadēva Rāya is evident from his inscriptions in the temple[1] Another epigraph[2] of Krishṇadēva Rāya says that while other gōpuras of the temple were the work of crowned kings the northern gopura was the work of God himself—a poetic way of saying that the northern gopura was the most beautiful. There is some evidence to suppose that the construction of the northern gōpura was undertaken by Krishṇadēva Rāya and was completed by his successor Achyuta Dēva Rāya.[3]

1 A R. E 371 of 1913
2 A R E 374 of 1913
3 I O R Vol XII, p 172

The eastern gōpura seems to have been built by Kōpperuñjiṅgadēva. 'According to an inscription at Tripurāntaka (Kurnool District) Mahārāja Sinba built the eastern gōpura and this king was evidently Kōpperuñjiṅgadēva.' It was renovated later by the mother-in-law of the great educational benefactor Pachaiyappa Mudaliār (1754-1794).[1] That the construction of the southern gōpura might have been undertaken by a Pāṇdya king may be inferred from the Pāṇdy crest—*the fish*—*on the cross stone* connecting the eastern and western walls of the gateway of the southern gōpura. The Attur inscription of Kōpperuñjiṅgadēva provides the revenues of certain villages for the superstructure of the southern gōpura in the form of a gōpura of seven storeys.

There is no specific epigraphic material as to the date of the foundation of the western gōpura. The niches in the west gōpura bear labels in the grantha script of the 13th Century A. D. and we may *take this to indicate that the gōpura must* have been built about the time. The earliest

---

1. Hamilton in his History of Hindustan observes that the eastern gōpura was repaired by a devout widow, the mother in-law of Pachaiyappa Mudaliar of Kañchipuram at the expense of 50,000 pagodas

The stone images of both Pachaiyappa and the lady are in the niches of the southern wall of the gateway of the eastern gōpura Refer to the 'Select Papers, Speeches and Poems connected with Pachaiyappa Mudaliar edited by V. Krishnamachariar (1892) wherein Mahāvidwan Sabhāpathi Mudaliar has sung of the rebuilding of the gōpura by Pachaiyappa in the last years of his life

literary references to the Karpavināyakar temple adjoining the western gōpura are found in Koyil-purānam [1]

The 100 pillared mandapa was built by Naralōkavīra one of the chiefs of the time of Vikrama Chōla [2] We have no epigraphic record for the construction of the 1000-pillared-mandapa But from the point of view of its architecture, it is ascribed to the Vijayanagar period

---

1 The following stanzas are found in Koilpuranam of Umapathi Sivāchārya and we may therefore take these references to confirm the existence of the Karpavināyakar temple and the western gōpura long before the 13th Century

[illegible]

[illegible]

[illegible]

"[illegible]

[illegible]"

2 A R E 1[illegible]0 of 1888

CHAPTER IV

HISTORY OF THE TEMPLE AS REVEALED BY ITS EPIGRAPHY

I

The ancient name of Chidambaram is Tillai. It is known by this name both in early literature and in epigraphs It was at first a forest of Tillai (Excoecaria Agallocha) trees. The other names by which Chidambaram is referred to both in Tamil literature, and in epigraphs are Puliyūr, Perumbaṟṟapuliyūr and Siṟṟambalam. Siṟṟambalam has been interpreted by the Government Epigraphist as 'the small temple as distinguished' from Pērambalam.' On the other hand Siṟṟambalam is taken to mean the place of 'Chit' *i.e.* divine knowledge.[1] The name Vyāgrapura which is a

---

1. "Chit means the subtile essence of the deity, filling all space. Being connected with the concrete term 'ambaram', the meaning of the term may be the essence of the spiritual symbol, 'spiritual soul' Ēkāmbara is a name of Śiva but Chitambara ignores visible form and this term was given to the first Saiva fane in South India having a sanctuary open to the heavens and without any idol," (Taylor Mss, Vol I, p 659)

"Chidambarēśvara and Chitsabhēśa have come into vogue as the result of the Sanskritisation of a distinctly Tamil word. The old name of the place in which the temple of this god now stands was Tillai or Tillaivanam. In Tillaivanam, there was evidently a temple of small propottions called Chiṟṟambalam or the small temple When the god of this temple became family deity of the

Sanskrit rendering of the Tamil name Puliyūr occurs in an inscription[1] of Rājēndra Chola III at Tirukannapuram which refers to the king as a worshipper at the divine lotus-feet of Kanakasabhāpathi at Vyāghrapura. The temple was so famous in ancient times that it is simply referred to in inscriptions as Tirukkōil. Chidambaram according to available inscriptions seems to have had at first as many as 14 hamlets

---

Chōla kings, the temple began to receive much royal consideration Gradually 'the small temple' grew in size by the addition of successive kings of Prakaras and Gōpuras, Maṇdapas and tanks and so on, still it retained the old name of Chirrambalam It is in fact praised in song as Chirrambalam by Tiruñānasambandar and Appar and also by the much later Sundaramurthi The popular pronounciation of this word Chirrambalam is generally Chittambalam ,and this became quite easily sanskritised in form to Chidambaram Therefore the Linga worshipped in the temple is conceived to represent the element akaśa or ether There is yet another modification which Chirrambalam underwent in the hands of such sanskritisers of Tamil names, and that is into the form Chitsabha The word Ambalam in Tamil means a hall which is translatable into Sanskrit as Sabha Thus arose Chitsabha and the god therein became Chitsabhēśa Thus the two names Chidambarēśvara and Chitsabhēśa came into existence thus also must have arisen the association of the Sphaṭika linga of the temple with these names (Hindu Iconography—Gopinatha Rao)

It is impossible to render Chit in English by any single word which would convey adequately all that is implied by this technical term We must therefore retain it untranslated

1 A R E 515 of 1922

II

Though the Chidambaram temple contains a large number of Sanskrit and Tamil inscriptions[1] there is no epigraphic evidence for the exact period when the temple was founded. For the period subsequent to the 10th century A. D. there is a good deal of epigraphic material, but for the period prior to the 10th century we have to depend largely upon literary tradition and folklore. Tradition has it that the Golden Hall was first built by Hiraṇya-varman, probably a Pallava king during the 6th century A. D. The reference in Tirumangai Alwar's songs to a Pallava king having made costly dedications to the Viṣṇu Shrine, and the reference in the works of Kulasēkhara and Tirumangai Maṉṉar to lofty walls of the shrine, and to the worship in Viṣṇu Shrine being conducted by the Dīkshitars make it certain that the two shrines of of Śiva and Viṣṇu were coeval in their times. There is also a small shrine for Brahma in the temple. It is therefore certain that the temple was founded at a time when the people had equal reverence for the three gods of the Hindu trinity—Brahma, Viṣṇu and Śiva—persumably during the Pallava period. The two important shrines of Naṭarāja and Govindarāja are situated in one and the same enclosure, and though they are in a common enclosure, the Naṭarāja shrine is the larger and more important institution in Chidambaram.

---

1. About 230 inscriptions of the temple have so far been deciphered. *Vide* Appendix.

The earliest epigraphical evidence[1] relating to the Naṭarāja temple is the inscription belonging to the 24th year of Rājēndra Chōla Dēva I (1018—1035 A. D.). The Leyden Grant refers to the Golden Hall which Parāntaka I (907—940 A. D.) is said to have covered with gold. From the fact that Māṇikkavāsagar refers to 'Poṉṉambalam' and 'Tillai Kūttan' in his works, it is quite certain that the temple must have come into existence before the 10th century A. D. when the Chōlas came into prominence.[2] There must have been an old Pallava shrine of which traces no longer exist owing to the complete renovation and additions made during the Chōla period. The Pallavas were great temple builders and a great many stone temples came into existence in the 7th Century A. D.[3]

The temple must have been one of small proportions prior to the Chōla period. It was during the time of the mediaeval Chōlas that the temple began to receive much royal consideration

---

1. A. R. E. 117 of 1888.
2. The Age of Maṇikkavāsagar is still disputed. It ranges from the 3rd to the 9th Century A D *Vide* Smith's Early History of India p. 247 M Srinivasa Iyengar—Tamil Studies (1914) pp. 401–409: Professor S. Krishnaswami Aiyangar—Ancient India pp. 321–22; K. A Nilakanta Sastri—Pandyan Kingdom p 63 foot note. As the poet saint ascribes an inferior position to Viṣṇu it is argued that the claims by Saivite Hagiologists to ascribe a very ancient date to Manikkavāsagar cannot be accepted as accurate.
3. Smith: Oxford History of India, pp 209-210 Venkayya: Monograph on Pallavas in Archaeological Survey of India.

Most of the Chōla kings were Śaivites and when the Śaivite God of this temple became their family deity, the temple grew in size by the additions of Prakāras, Gōpuras, Mandapas etc Almost all the important additions made during the Chōla and post-Chola period were made specifically in honour of Nataraja's shrine and there are no grants to the shrine of Govindarāja until we come to the Vijayanagar period. The walls of the two innermost squares of the temple are of Chola origin A number of inscriptions relating to the Chōla period refer to the prakāra walls of these enclosures as Kulōttunga Śōlan-tirumāligai and Vikrama Śōlan-tirumāligai.

The earliest Chōla kings who built or rebuilt various portions of the temple were staunch Śaivites The Thirumalvadi inscription [1] refers to the construction of portions of the temple by Vikrama-Chōla and the valuable gifts he made to the temple in the 10th year of his reign (1128 A D) He is said to have covered with gold the enclosure, the gate towers, halls and buildings surrounding the Ponnambalam Vikrama was succeeded by his son Kulōttunga II who reigned as Yuvaraj before 1134 A D and afterwards as sole king The famous court poet Ottakūthan has sung an Ulā on Kulōttunga II describing the services done to the temple. In the Ulā he refers to the building of Pērambalam, Gōpuras Māligais (walls) the seven storeyed Gōpuram, the shrine of Sivakāmi Sundari and the planning of the four streets round the temple The Ulā is a conventional composition of

1 South Indian Inscriptions, Vol III, Part II pp 183-86

the court-poet celebrating his master's triumph and must have been an exaggerated statement of the doings of the king, but the point is that epigraphy and contemporary literature point to the conclusion that the temple in its present form was mostly due to the munificence of the Chōla kings.

We may now refer in some detail to some of the important inscriptions of the temple and the historical events revealed by them. The inscriptions give us the names of some of the Chōla, Paṇdiya and Vijayanagar kings and also record some of the achievements of these rulers. The numerous inscriptions of the temple relate chiefly to gifts of land, jewels, cash etc. to the temple.

III

CHIDAMBARAM IN CHŌḺA TIMES

Though the names of some of the kings are repeatedly mentioned in several inscriptions, there are three inscriptions which give us the names of three Chōla princesses—Kundavi, Ammangai and Madurāntaki. The first of these princesses is called "Rajarajan Kundavi,—the younger sister of Kulōttunga-sōra-dēva (or Rajēndra Sōra-dēva)" and may be identified with Kundava [1], the daughter of Rājarāja; the second princess is referred to as "Ammangai, the daughter of Kulottunga-sōra-dēva" [2] and is identified with Ammangadēvi who married Rājarāja I; the third princess is referred to as "Madurantaki, the younger sister of our Lord

---

1 Epi. Indica, Vol IV p' 302; Ind Antiquary Vol. XIV p. 50.

2 South Indian Inscriptions, Vol. IV No 226.

(Kulōttunga Sōra-dēva)" One of the inscriptions of Vīrarājendra, the predecessor of Kulottunga I tells us that he presented a fine ruby called Trailōkyasara for being mounted on the crown of the Dancer of the Golden Hall The mediaeval Chōlas whose inscriptions are found in the temple are Kulōttunga I, Vikrama Chōla, Kulōttunga III and Rājarāja III.

One of the most interesting events of the temple frequently referred to in the inscriptions of the period is the work of covering the temple with gold, and this is claimed by various kings According to the Leyden Grant, Parāntaka I (A D 907–948) covered the Śiva temple at Chidambaram with gold,[1] and the credit of this work is also claimed for Kundavai[2] Parāntaka I's covering with gold the small hall (Dabhra sabha) which is a translation of Tamil Siṟṟambalam) of Śiva at Chidambaram is referred to in verse 53 of the Tiruvālangādu plates[3] Though tolerant of all religious in his dominions, he is known to have followed the Śaiva creed, as he utilised all the booty he acquired in his wars in covering with gold the temple at Chidambaram. We may refer in this connection to Gandar Āditya's Tiruviśaippa on Kōyil.[4] But there are no inscriptions of Parāntaka I in the temple itself to commemorate the achievements which are claimed for him

1 Archaeological Survey of India, Vol IV p 203

2 Epi Indica, Vol V p 105

3 Archaeological Survey of India Report, 1904–05 p 134

4 "தென்னாடும் ஈழமும் கொண்டதிறற் செங்கோற் சோழன் கோழிவேந்தன் செம்பியன் பொன்னணிந்த தில்லையம்பலத்தே."

Vikrama Chōla, the son and successor of Kulōttunga I who, though crowned king in A.D. 1118, was practically the ruler during the latter part of the reign of Kulōttunga I, is said to have covered the temple with gold. The Kulōttungan-Sōlan-Ulā, a Tamil poem composed in honour of Kulōttunga II says that Kulōttunga II covered the Naṭarājā temple at Chidambaram with gold. On the other land, the Rājarājan-Ulā, another Tami poem composed in honour of Rājarāja II, the sor of Kulōttunga II claims the act for its hero.

An inscription from Tiruppālaivaṉam[1] refers Tribhuvana Chakravartin Kulōttunga Chōla who covered with gold the temple at Pērambalam (Chidambaram). Another record[2] from the same place begins with the words 'Tiruppērambalam-pon-Vēiñdaruliya' Rajakēsari Varman. Both these inscriptions are attributed to Kulōttunga Chōla II whose claim to have covered with gold the temple at Chidambaram is known through other epigraphic[3] and literary references.

On the other hand, there are two incriptions of Vikrama Chola[4] which attribute this pious work to him. In fact, in an introduction of Vikrama-Chōla beginning with the words 'Pūmālaimidaindu'[5] this pious act is claimed by him. Another record

---

1. A R. E 349 of 1928-29.
2. A. R. E. 315 of 1928-29.
3. A. R E 330 of 1927
4. A. R E 165 of 1894 and 82 of 1895
5. A R. E 160 of 1894 and S I I. Vol. V, p 227 .

(350 of 1927) claims the act of covering the Ponnambalam *i.e.* Chidambaram temple with gold (sheets) for Tirubhuvanachakravartin Kulōttunga-Chola. Probably Vikrama-Chōla actually performed the act while Kulōttunga II merely adopted the title. Śēkkilār in his Periyapurānam mentions that Anapaya gilded the Chidambaram temple. Anapaya is known to be the surname of Kulōttunga II and and he had also pretensions to this meritorious deed. Thus the work of covering the temple with gold is claimed by various kings. But as a matter of fact some of the Devāram hymns which belong to an earlier date refer to the temple as செம்பொன்னில் எழுதிமேய்ந்த சிற்றம்பலம் பொன்னம்பலம். Which Chōla king had the better right to claim to himself the gilding of the temple is a question to which no conclusive answer can be given. But what is more important is that the way in which this event is recorded in Tamil literature and epigraphical records serves to establish the succesion of Chōla kings during this period.

An inscription on a pillar[1] in the outermost prakara to the north of the east gōpura in the Natarāja temple now fixed in the outermost east prakāra states that the mandapa (which must have contained this pillar) was constructed by Akalankan *i.e.* Vikrama-Chōla. The benefactions of this king to the temple are described in the historical introduction commencing with the words Pumalai midaindu perfacing his incriptions wherein God Natarāja is extolled as his family diety.[2] We

1 A R E 109 of 1935

2 The Cholas by K A Nilakanta Sastri Vol II (Pt I), pp 65, 66

know from inscriptions that the tirumāḷigai i the north side of the scond prakāra of the Chidam baram temple, the west entrance leading into th samo prakāra and the 100-pillared maṇḍapa wer constructed during his time and tho broken pilla may have belonged to any of these structures or t a different construction altogether of which w have no knowledge now.

Recent researches have brought to light th doings of the remarkable Chōla chieftain, Naralō kavira, in the days of Kulottunga I and his so Vikrama Chōla.[1] He is described by many name and titles in his inscriptions, such as Kaḷingarāja Sabhānātaka, Mānavatāra, Arulakāra, Naralōkovīra etc. There are about a dozen inscriptions bearing on the life and work of Naralōkavīran, and one o his inscriptions is found in Chidambaram. While most of his inscriptions make it appear that he was a mighty warrior, the inscription at Chidambaram shows that he used his great position and influence in the state in the service of religion. The most notable of his structures in Chidambaram on behalf of his master Vikrama-Chōladēva was the hall with a hundred pillars. A record[2] from Chidambaram in Tamil verse contains a catalogue of gifts made to the Natarāja temple.

---

1. A R. E. 1922 p. 115, K. A Nilakanta Sastri—Studies in Chola History and Administration.
2. A. R. E. [illegible];
   " தில்லையில் பொன்னம் பலத்தைச
   செம்பொனால்—மெருவர செல்லை
   யைப் பொக சாகி ... ...
   நூற்றுக் கால் மண்டபத்தே

The next Chōla ruler whose works at Chidambaram are of more of than ordinary interest is Kulōttunga II, the son and successor of Vikrama Chōla In one inscription it is claimed that he was 'the king who wore the crown is such wise as to add lustre to Tillainagai [1] Kulōttunga II's renovation of the temple is attested both by inscriptional records of his seventh year and literary works A detailed account of the remodelling of the temple by Kulōttunga II is given by Kulōttunga-sōlan-ulā and he is said to have constructed gōpurams with seven tiers and the shrine of the goddess, and the various parts of the temple are said to have been covered with gold Another famous Chōla whose inscriptions of the temple are helpful is Kulōttunga III (1178-1216) The latest date of Kulōttunga III is the 39th year in a manuscript at Chidambaram.[2] Kulōttunga III is known by other names—Vīrarājendra-solan-deva was one of his names and we learn from inscriptions of the temple that he was called Virarājendra-deva [3] The records of the reign of Kulōttunga III are numerous Four inscriptions[4] of the Chidambaram temple relating to Kulōttunga III are of particular interest Of

---

தில்லைப் பிரானுக்குச் செய்தமைத்தான்

புடைக்கணிகல சாந்து வித்தான்

வீதிகளும் கலவிளக்கிம விளக்கும வீற்றிருக்க

மண்டபமும மாது குழ

பாதமும மகுழ தோரகும, பொருளும திவலைசெ செய்தான"

1 155 of 1902

2 S I Inscriptions Vol III—Part I (1809) p 43

3 S I Inscriptions Vol III, p 205

4 A R E 121 of 1888 122 of 1888 457 of 1902 458 of 1902

these two relate to the 5th year and two to the 9th and 11th year respectively. All these inscriptions have a historical introduction, but the historical introduction of the inscriptions of the 5th year does not contain any statement of historical interest. The inscriptions of the 9th and 11th years contain statement of historical interest. The inscription of the 9th year relates 'how Kulōttunga III assisted Vikrama-Pāṇḍya against the son of Vira-Pāṇḍya, defeated the Marava army, drove the Sinhālese army into the sea, and took Madurai (Madura) from Vīra-Pāṇḍya and bestowed it to Vikrama Paṇḍya. The inscription of the 11th year refers' to the defeat of the son of Vīra Pāṇḍya and to the bestowal of Kūdal on Vikrama Pāṇḍya and adds that Vira-Pāṇḍya revolted again, but that Kulōttunga III 'took his crowned head.' Chidambaram is refered to in this inscription as Perumbāṟṟapuliyur in Rajādhirājan Valanādu and the temple as Tiruchchiṟṟambalam-udaiyar.

Kulōttunga-Chola III is again represented by three inscriptions from Chidambaram. Two of these[1] with the introduction Puyalvāyattu etc. and in his 7th year call him Vīrarājendra dēva. The inscription from Chidambaram gives some interesting glimpses of land transactions associated with their grant to the temple In one of these[2] two persons Vijayarājan of Velur in Rājēndrasoḷa-vaḷanaḍu, Ponnnamudan of Śiṟkudi in Uyyakoṇḍār-vaḷanādu purchased some plots of land for forming

1. A.R E. 3 and 4 of 1936.
2. A. R E. 3 of 1936

a flower-garden to the temple in four villages from the mūlaparishad of Perumbaṟṟapuliyūr in the name of a certain Kavuśiyan Mahēśvaran Kumaran of Mituṉikkudi. These lands comprised two kinds, taramperra (assessed) and taramili or aḷavil-nīngāl (not assessed) The taramili lands were utlised for guhai for the tapasvins and as site for the flower-garden The former kind, viz. those entered in the accounts as assessed lands from which taxes were being realized by the assembly hitherto, were endowed by the donors for the upkeep of the garden, and on their petition to the king, the taxes due thereon were henceforth remitted and so entered in the accounts of Varikku-Kūṟuśeyvaṉ (assessing officer?) The four tenants looking after the flower-garden were also exempted from the Kudimai taxes. All the concerned documents were to be deposited in the temple treasury. This document was issued over the signature of eight officers under the orders of the king. Almost the same kind of transaction is recorded in an epigraph[1] dated a few months later and in another epigraph[2] dated in the 11th year of Kulōttunga-Chōla-dēva In all these transactions the lands were purchased by the donors not in their own names from the original owners nor in the name of the temple to which the endowment was made but in the name of some entirely different individual. The reason for this procedure is not clear from the contents of the inscriptions. It is interesting to note that among the owners

1. A. R. E 4 of 1936.
2. A R E. 7 of 1936.

mentioned in the records from whom the lands were purchased by the donor figures a certain Dāmōdiraṉ Iruṇdanārāyana-Bhaṭṭan of Māriṅgūr who is referred to as a teacher (or purohita?) depending upon the village for his maintenance (grāmāśrayam-irukkumuvātti).

According to the information in some of the epigraphs about the building operations of Kulōttunga III[1] we learn that he built the 'mukha-maṇdapa of Sabhāpathi and gōpura of the shrine of the goddess Girindrāja and the enclosing verandah (Prakāraharmya). These references are to the Natarāja temple at Chidambaram, where the king must have built the 'mukha-maṇdapa' the 'gōpura' of the shrine of the goddess Śivakāmi Amman and the verandah enclosing the central shrine. Kulōttunga III is also described as an unequalled devotee (ēkhabakta) of the God at Chidambaram.

Of Rājarāja III, there are several inscriptions from Chidambaram. One of them[2] registers an endowment for a flower garden to the god after its purchase from the Mūla-parishad of Perumpaṟṟup-puliyur by Sōmanātha Dēva *alias* Udaiyūr Svāmi Devar Saṇdilya-gōtra who hailed from the Uttarāgrahāra in Uttara-rāshtra of Uttarapātha. The donor is referred to at the end of the inscription in respectful terms and hence he seems to have been a very influential person at the time and probably the religious head of some matha at the place. Rājarāja's other inscriptions record mostly

1. A. R. E 190, 191 and 192 of 1908.
2 A. R. E. 9 of 1936

gifts of lands made after purchasing them, to the temple at Chidambaram which was made tax-free by order of the king One of the records[1] mentions certain lands which were in the enjoyment of Velichchēri Savarnan Gautaman Śvāmi Kumaraṉ Arulalabhattaṉ *alias* Savarna—Chakravarthi of Uttamasōlamangalam in Rajadhirāja-valanādu from the 12th year of the king and which was now purchased from his sons by a certain lady for being endowed to the temple

IV

CHIDAMBARAM IN PANDYA (MEDIAEVAL) TIMES

There are no epigraphs in the temple relating to the early Pāndyas All the available epigraphs relate to the mediaevel Pāndyas who rose to power about the end of the reign of the Chōla King Kulōttunga I An inscription of Māravarman Sundara Pāndya I[2] (acc 1216) gives a fairly complete account of the king's achievements up to the 8th year of his reign in which it is dated He is said to have set fire to Tañjai (Tanjore) and Urandai (Uraiyur), to have demolished numerous halls, ramparts, towers and pavilions there, to have driven the Sembiyan (Chōla king) into the forest, and to have performed the anointment of heroes in a pavilion at Āyirattalāi The king after having worshiped Nataraja at Puliyur (Chidambaram) proceeded to Pon-Amarapati, and while staying there in his big palace, he summoned the Chōla king to his presence promising to give him

1 A R E 8 of 1936

2 A R E 2 of 1920

back his country (i.e Sōnadu) and his crown Thereupon the Chōla king (i e Rājirāja III) came in all humility in obedience to this mandate and prostrated before him, and the Pāndya king restored the Chōla to his dominions

A number of epigraphs[1] record gifts to the temple and refer to the victories Hoysala (Sōmēsvara) Gandagōpa, the Kakatiya king (Ganapati) and the king of Cuttack, Malabar and Ceylon The value of these historical references lies in the fact that they help us to identify this king as Jatavarman Sundara Pāndya I who ruled from A D 1251-61. The eastern and western main gopuras of the temple contain some epigraphs[2] referring to the achievements of a certain Sundara Pāndya who has been identified as Jatavarman Sundara Pāndya I One of these inscriptions contains two verses, the first verse referring to the conquest of the Chōla by the Pāndya king and the second verse mentions Kādavarkōn (Pallava king) and the Pāndya king, Sundaratōl. Two other inscriptions[3] praise the military prowess of Sundara Maran (i e Sundara Pāndya) who defeated the Telungas at Mudugūr One of the inscriptions (354 of 1913) consists of three Tamil verses describing the glory of Sundara Pāndya who conqured the king of Venadu (i e Travancore) the Telungas and the Kongu country and killed Ganda-gōpāla The value of these inscriptions of Sundara Pāndya I

1 A R E 170, 171, 172, 173 176 to 184 of 1892, Ind Ant. Vol XXI pp 122 and 343

2 A R E 332, 340 and 361 1913

3 A R E 340, 361 of 1913

consists in confirming some of the achievements claimed for that ruler as a great warrior. Some of the inscriptions[1] of the temple refer to Sundara Pāndya I's weighing himself against gold; and he is also credited with having built a golden hall at Chidambaram.[2]

Another epigraph[3] referring to Jatavarman Sundara Pāṇdya I records the agreement by the trustees of the Tiruvanantēśvarasvāmin and Nāyanār Mannanār temple situated between the Kollidam and Vellaru rivers that certain dues on lands in the village belonging to the temple at Chidambaram should be remitted and that the amount should be rateably enhanced on the remaining lands in the village The popularity of this king, Sundara Pāndya I was commemorated by the inauguration of several religious and civic charities. A record from Chidambaram[4] registers the establishment of a grove and an avenue of coconut trees planted on either side of it for the recreation and habitation of the people

There are a few epigraphs[5] of Jatavarman Vira Pāṇdya which refer to him as one who took Ilam (Ceylon) Kongu and the Śolamandalam (i.e the Chōla country) and who having conquered the the powerful (Chōla) king was pleased to perform the anointment of heroes and victors at Perumbārrappuliyur (i e Chidambaram) and this king is

1 A R E 338 and 363 1913
2 S I I Texts Vol IV, Nos 627 and 630
3 A R E 535 of 1920
4 A R E 546 of 1919
5 A R E 131 of 1907 437 of 1917 Refer 192 of 1914 of Jaṭavarman Vira Pāṇdya

perhaps identical with the Vīra-Pāṇḍyā whose initial date according to Kielhorn is A. D. 125[illegible] We also learn from other sources that Jaṭa-varman Vīra Pāṇḍya encamped at Chidambaram to collect tribute from his subordinates and to perform the 'Abhiṣēka'.

There are some epigraphs of Vikrama Pāṇḍya in Chidambaram which serve to set in a clear light the doings of that ruler by confirming the conclusions derived from other sources. He is referred to by his titles Bhūvaṇika Vīra and Koṛkai Kāvala, and of having conquered the Vēnādu (*i.e.* Travancore) king at Podiyil. One of the epigraphs[1] is of particular interest. It consists of six verses in Tamil of which five refer to a battle fought at Chidambaram (apparently on the banks of Veḷḷāṛu near Chidambaram) by a certain Munaiyan Valliyan Ādittan, chief of Panaiśeyyar on behalf of the Pāṇḍya (Miṉavaṉ) against the Chōla (Vaḷavaṉ). The author of the poem was Tāynalla-Perumal Munaiyadaraiyan *alias* Bhūvaṇikavīra Toṇḍaimān It may be noted that there is a dim historic truth underlying these references, though the historical details claimed by these epigraphs may be a highly overdrawn picture.

There are several epigraphs in the Chidambaram temple,[2] referring to Maravarman Vīra Pāṇḍya and they suggest the possibility of this king being the successor of Maravarman Vikrama Pāṇḍya, and also the contemporary of Ravivarman Kulasēkhara. That a part of the South Arcot came

1 A. R. E. 329 of 1913

2 A. R. E. 279, 320, 328, 3[illegible]1 and 386 of 1913, 5 of 1936

into the temporary possession of a ruler of Kērala, Kulasēkhara in the early part of the 14th century is evident from one of the epigraphs in the Chidambaram temple.

V

From the latter half of the 12th century, the Chōla power become more and more weak and there were also signs of decay among the Pāṇdyas. The times were thus highly favourable for feudatories to rise into prominence. For instance, the Sambuvarayans who held a subordinate position under the Chōlas and had done signal service to them under four successive sovereigns Rājarāja II, Rajādhirāja II, Kulōttunga III and Rājarāja III new began to assert themselves. There are numerous inscriptions of the later Pallava chieftains who held away in South Arcot. Most prominent among the chiefs who took advantage of the weakness of the Chōlas in the 13th century was Kōpperuñjingadēva. He asserted his independence and ruled for about 36 years from A D. 1243 to at least 1278-79,[1] and it is evident from some epigraphs that his dominions extended southward beyond the Coleroon into the Tanjore District. He bore the titles 'Sakala bhuvana Chakravartin,' the emperor of all the worlds and 'Āvāṇi-āḷappirandan *i.e.* one who was born to rule the earth.' Some of Kōpperuñjinga's epigraphs are found in the Naṭarāja temple and the Tillai Amman temple at Chidambaram. These epigraphs mention some of his chief officers, notably Perumal Pillai *alias* Śōlakaṉ, Teṉṉavaṉ

1. Epi. Indica, Vol. VII, p. 105

Brahmādhirājan, 'Jayatuṅga-Pallavarayan, and Tillai Ambalappallavarayan. The earliest references to the local Tillai Amman temple are to be found in the inscriptions of Kōpperuñjingan and one of the inscriptions[1] is of particular interest, as it refers to the 'temple (Śrikōil) of the Pidāri called Tiruchiṟṟambala Mākāḷi.' Mr. Krishna Sastri has pointed out that, according to an inscription at Tirupurantaka (Kurnool District) a certain king Mahārāja Sinha built the eastern gōpura of the Naṭarāja temple and that 'the king was evidently Kōpperuñjingadēva Three pillars[2] for the merit of his master-Peruñjingadeva—one on the west entrance into the second prakara of the temple, one on the gōpura at the main entrance into the Śivakāmi Amman shrine, and one now found on the door-post of a new entrance close to the eastern gōpura—were set up by Śoḷakan for the merit of his master Kōpperuñjinga's donations to the temple and his devotion to the god at Chidambaram are evidenced by the epigraphs as well as by his title—Kanakksabhāpathi–Sabhā arvakaiya-arvakala-Nirvahakah.[3]

Peruñjingadēva had several surnames–Aḷagiya-Pallavan, Śokkachchīyan Śokkachchīyan-kōl and Śokkachchīyan-tirunandavanam (103 of 1935) indicate that Śokkachchīyan was another title of his. It is interesting to note from the record[4]

---

1 A R E 312 of 1913

2. A. R. E. 321, 324, 325 of 1913.

3. A. R E 418 of 1922, 286 of 1921; 197 of 1905. 419 of 1893 (dated in Saka 1184); 136 of 1900

4. A. R. E. 105 of 1935.

dated in the 19th year of this chief, Kopperuñjingadēva that the donor Gaṅgōḷi Tiruchiṟṟambalamadaiyār *alias* Udaiyār Iśwara-Sivar of the Śavarna-gōtra who hailed from the Rādhā country (Bengal) in Uttarāpatha, formed a garden called Tiruchiṟṟambalam—Udaiyār—tirunandavanam at Chidambaram for the use of the temple. Another record[1] dated in the 36th year contains the order of the Mūlaparishad which was communicated to Tennavan Brahmādhirājan Jayatunga-Pallavaraiyar Tillaiambala-Pallavaraiyar and to the Mahēśwaras etc. of the temple of Tiruchiṟṟambalam Udaiyar by the king's officer Vēṇāḍudaiyāṉ exempting from taxes ten vēlis of land which had been formed into a hamlet called Tillaināyaka Chaturvēdamangalam and presented to the temple by Aḻagiya-Tiruvaiyārudaiyar belonging to the Tirunākkaraśu-ten-tirumadam situated in the street called 'Ambalanayāka-perunteruvu' The donation was made for meeting the expenses of several items *viz.* (1) chanting the Vēda outside the temple on the days when the god was taken out in procession in the car (2) chanting benedictory mantras on the days when the god halted in the garden called Kulōttungaśōlan-tirutōppu (3) for chanting the Vēdas during the service of the sacred bath of the god, (4) for the ceremony of Mṛitgrahaṇa when the god (Piḷḷaiyar) Śivapādaśēkharan-sittaitu-tuṇaip-perumāḷ was taken for circumambulating the pālikai in the garden called Edirīśōlan-tirunandavanam and (5) for providing cake offerings on the days when the image of Kulōttungaśola-Vināyaka-piḷḷaiyār, whose shrine is located in the eastern

1. A. R. E. 104 of 1935

portion of the temple is taken in procession to the street called Rājākkaḷtambiran-tiruvīdi. This inscription was ordered to be engraved on the 'Vikramaśōlan-tirumāḷigai' and near the inscription relating to some gift made to the Brahmans of Irumarabuntivyaperumāḷ-Chaturvēdamangalam, a hamlet of Koṟṟavangudi.

VI

Before passing on to the Vijayanagar period, we may refer to a few institutional features revealed by the inscriptions of the temple. It is clear from the incriptions that all gifts of land made to the temple had to be engraved on the walls of the temple. In Śiva temple all transactions connected with the temple were done in the name of Chandeśvara who is expressly stated to be the first servant of God. It was in his name that the sale and purchase of temple lands took place. Up to the time of Vikrama Chōla, all transactions made on behalf of the Chidambaram temple were made in the name of Chandeśvara but subsequently they were registered in the name of the temple priests and trustees either jointly or severally. This may be taken to refer to the time when the Mūlasthāna-shrine and the image of Chandeśvara by its side was considered to be the sanctum sanctorum of the temple. The prominence given to the Naṭaraja shrine in later inscriptions accounts for the disappearance of Chandeśvara and the substitution in his place of one of the temple committee. This change suggests the reason why at the present day the Dīkshitars of Chidambaram have come to be the practical owners of the temple. In the days of

Kulōttunga III, the order of the king or of his officers which was written by his royal secretary (Tirumandira Olai) was generally addressed to the executive members of the temple assembly, the temple priests, the managing committee and the supervisors of the temple. A large number of Kulōttunga III's officers are mentioned in the inscriptions as also those of Kōpperunjinga The original title-deeds of lands granted to the temple and other connected documents such as the resolution of the village assembly to make the land rent-free or receiving some fixed amount from the donor (290 of 1913) or to distribute the due tax on other assessed lands of the village (280 of 1913) had to be deposited in safe custody in a room or office of the temple called tirukkaiottipaṇḍāram.

It is desirable to refer to a few inscriptions of the temple which are of interest to the student of village economics and administration. That the revenue survey of the Tamil country was made from time to time by some of the kings is known to us from early epigraphs [1] An inscription of the Chidambaram temple [2] also confirms this fact by referring to a land survey in the 16th year of Kulōttunga I The existence of a land survey committee (nilam alavu padipperumakkal) [?] of the village assembly of Perumpārṟappuliyūr which functioned in respect of land revenue assessment of temple lands is attested by one of the Chidambaram epigraphs.[3] Another epigraph [4] gives minute

1 199 of 1917, 285 of 1918

2 317 of 1913

3 262 of 1913

4 457 of 190.

fractions of vēlis and land measures and is therefore of great interest to the student of economic history There was a regular survey of land (317 of 1913). Eight different classes of land are referred to in one of the Chidambaram inscriptions (262 of 1913)—the extent, ownership, assessment, classification, etc., had to be noted in village and temple registers by clerks specially appointed for the purpose. Registry in village books and enjoyment were considered essential to establish one's ownership in any property.

There are several epigraphs referring to the remission of assessments on lands granted to the temple. A record of Jaṭavarman Sundara-Pāṇḍya (289 of 1913) from Chidambaram contains an order for the remission of certain taxes on some lands which being close to the sea 'had become filled up with sand and overgrown with weeds.' We learn that the village assembly (mūla parushsiyar) dealt at times with the temple lands (288 and 296 of 1913). Original documents pertaining to gifts of land made to the temple were preserved in the treasury of the temple and engraved on its walls (298, 299, 306 and 309 of 1913) The royal order which made known these arrangements was known as 'Tirumandira Olai' (299, 310, 311 of 1913); the village accountants were known as 'Varaikāru Sevyar' (311 of 1913).

One of the inscriptions of Sundara Paṇḍyadēva on the south well of the first prakāra of the Natarāja temple[1] gives interesting details of the

1. 277 of 1913

founding of an agrahara named Vikrama-Pāndya Chaturvēdimangalam on the western side of Perumbarrappuliyūr and its presentation to 108 learned Brahmins. (For the maintenance of these and other village accessories (grâmaparikara) the village Rajāsikhamanimallur *alias* Puliyangudi on the western bank of Ponneri was acquired and granted, being divided into 147¾ share (paṅgu) The inscription is worth quoting in full, as it is one of the few inscriptions relating to the foundation of a new village

The village granted was Vikrama-Pāndya Chaturvēdimaṅgalam evidently after the name of an unknown brother or father (nāyanār) of Sundara Pāṇdya. In the centre of it was also established the temple of Vikrama-Pāndyēśvara similarly designated The village was intended to accomodate primarily 108 Brahmanas among whom were many well-versed in Vedas and Śastras and able to expound the same Four velis of land were purchased for the village site and included within it, the temple premises, the house sites of the 108 Brāhmanas mentioned above, of men whoever in charge of the village library (Sarasvati-bhanḍarattāi) and of the village servants (panimakkal). In purchasing the land with its trees, wells, paths, channels, embankments, indicating land divisions (bhājaś raya) and all other benefits, the rights and privileges of the old tenants and title-holders were completely bought up The right of way was secured for the Brāhmanas to walk to the tank Kāvarkulam every day for the purpose of performing Sandhyāvandana prayers Land for grazing the cattle was also provided for, also for the maintenance of the 108 Brāhmin families and others are acquired 117¾ vēlis of land in the village of Rājasikhāmaninallūr (*alias*) Puliyaṅgudi. The Brāhmanas evidently received each a full vēli of land. The following other vrittis were also settled:- teachers of the Vēdas 3; teachers of the sūtras 1; two doctors 1¾; *ambadayas? ½; carpenter ½ village accountant ½; drummer ¼; potter ¾; blacksmith ¼; goldsmith ¼; iraṅkolli ⅜; barber ¾; washerman ¼; village watchman (padi-kāppan) ¾; and the village servant (veṭṭiyan) ⅛. Of the natta land outside the agrahāra 'Braḥmai quarters', three parts were set apart for Vellān-Kāniyālar and the remainder for other profes-sionals?) The fruit-trees, gardens, ponds, water-pits, grazing grounds, irrigation channels, uncultivable waste, embankments (?) of fields and pathways included in the village site were made over (to the donees) as per customary law. All taxes were excused but it was stipulated that from the 14th year of the king 500 kalams of superior paddy was to be measured out every year to the temple at Chidambaram for conducting the Sandi, Ellāndalaian Perumāl Sandi and that all lands which belonged to temples (Tirunāmattuk kani) must be demarcated by stones marked with the trident. [1]

---

1. A. R E. 1914 Part II, Para 18

VII

CHIDAMBARAM IN VIJAYANAGAR DAYS.

Inscriptions of the Hindu dynasty of Vijayanagar are found all over South Arcot which formed a part of Tondaimandalam. There are several epigraphs relating to the Vijayanagara kings of the earlier and later dynasties. The earliest record is that of Devaraya II dated S. 1349 (A. D. 1428). An inscription [1] on the north wall of the Karpaga Vinayaka shrine in the western gopura of the temple records the fact that 'the king ordered certain irregularities in temples and temple lands to be set right.' The full text is worth quoting as it discloses the lines on which the temples were supported and their affairs were regulated by the king. The king's order ran as follows:

"As we have been informed by the Mahēśvaras and Marụdavanachchivan that the king's officers in the villages belonging to the temples are unjustly collecting the taxes called Kanikkai Arasuperu, Karanakkar-jodi, viseshadayam alamanji etc., representing these to be dues payable to the palace; that the villagers taking up on mortgage the lands purchased, presented or otherwise owned by the temples, stubbornly refuse to give back those lands to the temples and that as a consequence the temple tenants abandoned the villages causing thereby the stoppage of worship in these temples, we order that the taxes mentioned above shall no longer be collected, the only payable tax, however

1. A. R E. 376 of 1913, A R E 1914, p. 97.

being the Sūlavarippon, that the worship etc., in your temples shall be conducted in future under the direction of the said Marudavāṇachchivan and that temple lands shall in no case be let out on (long) lease, nor shall they be assigned to anyone as tax-free hereditary property, free gift or bhaṭṭavritti."

The next Vijayanagara King who has left a monument of his greatness in the Chidambaram temple is Krishnadeva Raya (1509—30). Important temples in Southern India such as those at Conjeevaram, Tirupati, Tiruvannamalai, and Chidambaram were visited by him on his tour of conquest, and received munficicent donations. The extent to which South Indian temples benefited at his hands in the shape of buildings, such as maṇḍapas, gōpuras and prākāras can be seen from the South Indian Inscriptions. In 1510 Krishnadeva Raya made a gift of three villages with an income of 1400 rēkai (gadyana) for the mahāpūja of Aḷagiya Tiruccirrambalam Udaiya Tambirāṇār.[1] The northern gopura of the Chidambaram temple was built by him in memory of his victories in the north[2] (S. 1438 *i. e.* about A D. 1516) One of these records registers the fact that Krishnadēva Rāya after having started on a campaign against Simhadri-Pottunūru planted a pillar of victory there, and returning thence, he paid a visit to Ponnambalam (*i. e.* Chidambaram,) worshipped the God and built the northern gōpura of the temple.

---

1 A. R. E 323 of 1913.

2. A. R E. 174 and 175 of 1892, 371 and 374 of 1913, vide S I. I. Vol. IV. Nos. 622 and 623 (Texts)

There is no specific gift of this great king of Vaishnavite sympathies to the Vishnu shrine in the temple and it is therefore resonable to infer that during his time the Govindaraja shrine had ceased to exist as an independent shrine in the temple.

Another epigraph on the eastern gōpura of the temple records the grant (S. 1443 *i. e.* A. D. 1522) of the village of Chidambaranathapuram to the temple by Maṅgaraśan who is persumed to be identical with Taraṇikka Maṅgaraśayyan, who was Viceroy of Krishnadēvaraya in Tiruvadi-rājya (South Arcot district).[1] A record[2] of Achyutadēva Mahārāya (dated in Śaka 1451) gives the names of 82 villages, the income from which amounting to 3000 poṇ had been originally alloted by Krishna Raya Nayaka for the expenses of the car and other festivals and for repairs to the temple at Perumbṟṟappuliyūr and was now endowed by the king at the instance of Saluva-Daṇṇāyaka.

The Govindaraja shrine in the inner enclosure of the temple has an eventful and chequered history. There are epigraphic and literary references. The epigrapical references are very few and all these belong to the Vijayanagar period.[3] The disproportionately small number of inscriptions relating to this shrine may be explained by the fact that this shrine attained to an independent

---

1. A. R. E. 333 of 1913
2. A R. E. 2 of 1936.
3. Rangacharya List of S. I. Inscriptions, Vol 1, pp. 131-33 and p. 149, Nos 63, 64 and 109 of which one is said to be spurious.

existence only in or about the middle of the 16th century A.D. But there is some evidence based upon contemporary traditional literature which goes to show that the shrine is of much earlier origin, and from such material we are able to reconstruct the early history of this shrine, prior to the 16th century A. D.[1] The earliest references to Govindarāja's shrine belong to a period anterior to the 10th century A. D. They are to be found in the Prabhandams of the two Alwārs Kulasēkhara and Tirumangai-maṉan.[2] It may be asked whether the material afforded by the two Alwārs affords sufficient basis for historical foundation of the Govindarāja's shrine prior to the 10th century A. D. Even if we assume the references in such literary tradition to be sufficient, it is argued that the shrine referred to in these Tamil works could not be identified with Govindarāja's shrine. In eleven verses Kulasekhara has sung in praise of Vishnu in Tiruchitrakūṭa and refers to the deity as Rama in a sitting posture. Tirumangai Alwār describes the deity as reclining on a serpant, and

---

1. Sen Tamil Vol. III, pp 164 to 170 and 298 to 302.
2. The exact age of these two Alwars is as unsettled as the age of Manikkavasagar Nevertheless it is certain that the said Alwars and Manikkavasagar belonged to a period anterior to the 10th century A. D According to Prof. S Krishnaswami Aiyangar in his History of Vaishnavism Kulasekhara's date is between the 6th century A. D. and the early part of the 11th century A. D An inscription of the 18th year of Kulottunga (1088) makes provision for the recital of Kulasekhara's works. This may be taken to mean that Kulasekhara became famous by that time. As regards Tirumangai Alwar, the same author places him in the latter half of the 8th century (Ancient India, pp. 322-23)

both refer to the same deity presumably, the former to the Utsavar (the metal idol) and the latter to the Mūlavar (the stone idol) In both cases the deity is described to have been worshipped according to Śastras by Thillai Mūvayiravars *i e* 3,000 Dikshitars of Thillai These references are interesting and may be taken to point to the management of the entire institution by the Dikshitars and we may infer that the Vishnu shrine had then no separate existence

• The reference to Govindarāja's shrine in Manikkavasagar's Tiruchchirrambala Kōvai is contained in stanza 86 and he says that Vishnu was lying in the *courtyard of* Thillai Ambalam supplicating Siva, when in response to Vishnu's prayer he showed *one foot that he might show the* other as well There are references to the shrine in four *other places* in *the poem* (stanzas 42 105, 132 and 157)

The next literary reference to the shrine of Govindaraja is to be found in Ottakūthan's Ulās and his work entitled Takkayagapparani In describing the various services rendered to the Nataraja temple by Kulōttunga II, the poet refers to the Vishnu shrine having been rooted out when the renovation of the temple was carried out. In another Ulā, the Vishnu god is said to have been submerged in the sea, his former abode. The reference in Takkayagaparani is to the effect that for finding a space for Thillai Manru (the temple of Thillai) the Vishnu God had to be forced back to his former abode - the sea In confirmation of this bigotry of Kulōttunga II mentioned by the court poet, we have an epigraphic record of (dated 14th year of his reign) which seems to open with the mention of the destruction of Vishnu shrine in Chidambaram.[1]

According to the Vaishnavite Guruparamparas, the Chitrakuta was destroyed in the time of Ramānuja[2] (1016-17 to 1137 A. D). The image of Govindarāja was removed by the Vaishnavas to Tirupati and consecrated there by Ramanuja. Kulōttuṅga II ruled from 1135 to 1146 and jointly with Vikrama Chōla from 1123 to 1135. So the removal of the idol from Chidambaram and its consecration at Lower Tirupati should have taken place some-where between 1123 and 1136. But the massive Muḷavar (idol in stone in a lying posture) must have been allowed to remain somewhere in the temple.

According to tradition Ramānuja was persecuted by a certain Chōḷa king by name Kulōttuṅga who demanded assent to his doctrine 'Sivat Pārataramnasti' -'(i.e there is no being (God) superior to Siva). So Ramānuja might have given up the idea of restoring Govindarāja shrine in Chidambaram which had by this time become the strong hold of Saivism by reason of the fact that not only Naṭarāja was the family deity of the Chōḷa kings but that Chidambaram was almost the seat of Chōḷa kings.

---

1. A R E 363 of 1907.
2. Rāmānuja lived in the last quarter of the 11th and first half of the 12th centuries A D. (V A. Smith: Oxford History, p 204, Imperial Gazetteer Vol. II p 254.

Whether Ottakūthan's description of Kulōttunga's vandalism is an interpolation or not has been a point of dispute. It may however be observed that when two sets of rival traditional literature are agreed as to this incident of the idol of Govindarāja being removed from the shrine, it is certain that the incident had actually taken place. This brings the history of the shrine to the middle of the 12th century A D

In this connection we may mention one or two sources of history traceable to this period which throw some light as to the exact significance of the royal wrath towards Govindarāja in Kulōttunga s time and the possible tolerant attitude adopted by kings subsequent to Kulōttunga II up the time of Achyuta Raya It is just possible that what was thrown was the small Utsavar idol which according to the usual practice obtaining when new temples are founded was taken to Lower Tirupati from an ancient shrine in Chidambaram just to enable the history of Lower Tirupati shrine to be traced back to the time of the Alwars and the large massive Mulavar idol was kept on one of the platforms that surrounded the temple The fact that the Vaishnavites were able to enshrine the God in Tirupati shows the limitation of Chōla authority or the fact that they were indifferent to it so long as the deity of Govindaraja was removed from the immediate vicinity of the family deity of the Chōlas,

The next literary reference to the shrine is in the time of Vedanta Deśika In the traditional account of Vedanta Deśika, the Vaishnavite apostle, there is a reference to the worship having been set up in Govindarāja's shrine with the aid of Gōpaṇṇarāya of Gingee. The Guruparamparai Prabhāvam seems to imply that Vedānta Dēśika had to act against the people of Chidambaram in restoring worship and took advantage of an internal commotion in the place to restore the image of Govindarāja.[1] It is a settled historical fact that Gōpaṇṇa and Kampaṇṇa were two of the lieutenants of Bukka, the able King of Vijayanagar and they played a leading part in putting down the precarious rule of the Muhamadans and establishing the sovereignty of Vijayanagar over a great portion of Southern India.[2] Gōpaṇṇa is stated to have been a staunch Vaishnavite. Many temples were rebuilt during this period of Hindu revival.

The earliest epigraphisal reference[3] in the temple is a record of the Vijayanagara king Achyutayya Mahārāyp (dated Ś 1461 i.e. A D. 1539) who ordered that the image of Tillai Govindarāja Perumāḷ at Perumbaṟṟappuliyūr might be set up according to the ritual of Vaikāṇasa Sūtra and granted 500 poṉ which was the income of four

---

1 J B BR. A S XXIV, p 309

2 The Chidambaram temple must also have been affected by the calamities of the Muhamadan domination during the 14th century (Eliot History of India, Vol III pp. 90 91) In 1311 Malik Kafur invaded South India and plundered among the other places Brahmastapuri which is identified with Chidambaram by Prof. S Krishnaswami Iyengar This identification needs further research and involves some controversy

3 A. R. E 272 of 1913 1 of 1915

villages for the upkeep of daily worship Whether the act of Achyuta was a consecration or a reconsecration has been a subject of some controversy. The reconsecration theory lends support to the contention that Govindarāja was in existence in this temple even prior to Achyuta's time It has been argued that prior to the time of Achyuta Raya the existence of the image of Govindarāja has to be inferred from tradition and religious literature and that the idol appears to have occupied one of the mandapams in the Thirumaligaipatti (platform near the wall) round Natarāja's shrine.

Whether Govindarāja's idol existed previous to the days of Achyuta Raya or whether the image was newly set up, the only way of describing the royal act of Achyuta Raya would be to call it a consecration according Vaikhānasa ritual. The whole tenor of Achyuta Raya's order would indicate that Vaikhānasa ritual was first introduced in his time It also appears from inscriptions (Nos 546 and 548 of 1918) that in order to build a Vimana in front of Govindarāja's shrine and to open an entrance, an old Chōla wall was broken open. The broken fragments must have formed a continuous inscription before the opening of the gate. The opening of a separate entrance to the sanctum sanctorum of Govindarāja must have been done as a sort of compromise between the votaries of Visnu and Śiva who by this period must have developed considerable sectarian feelings Before the opening of this new entrance and the establishment of the worship according to Vaikhānasa ritual both the shrines must have been under one and the same management and ritual.

The only other reference to the shrine of Govindarāja is to be found in a work entitled Prapannamritam. The author of this work attributes the honour of consecration to Mahācharya or Doddācharya of Shōlinghur who was able to achieve his object with the aid of Rama Raya who ruled after Krishnadevaraya. Here is therefore a difficult problem of reconciliation of tradition with history. According to one writer[1] this Rama Raya died in the battle of Talikota (1565) and the restoration of the shrine must have been prior to 1565 A. D. On the other hand, it is argued[2] that the first inscription of Achyutaraya's time (1569) would support the version of Prapannamritam, if Rama Raya is taken to be a mistake for Achyutaraya. If not, there must have been another attempt to remove the idol after Achyuta's time and a final restoration of it by Mahācharya in the 16th century A. D. A careful reading of the expression used in Prappannamritam would show that the Prapannamritam refers to the same incident as is referred in the inscription of Achyuta's time. The expression used in Prápannamritam means that Rama Raya was a king who ruled after the famous king Krishnadevaraya. This does not necessarily mean that Rama Raya was Krishnadevaraya's immediate succesor. Rama Raya was the son-in-law of Krishnadevaraya and must have been famous in Achyuta's time. Achyuta was a feeble monarch and after his death the Empire fell into the hands of Rama Raya while

---

1. Prof. S. Krishnaswami Aiyangar. Ancient India, p 230
2. V. Rangachari's List of inscriptions Vol, I, p 133.

Sadāśiva was the nominal ruler.[1] It is therefore likely that popular tradition attributes the honour to Rama Raya instead of Achyuta Raya.

There is another possible reconciliation of tradition with history. It is just possible that Achyuta Raya ordered on the said date and determined upon the consecration But the actual carrying out of the order might have been done a few years later by Rama Raya The Prapannamrita mentions that the Śaivite scholars of Chitrakūta had to be defeated by Mahācharya before he conceived the idea of restoring worship in the shrine. Among such scholars was the famous Appayya Dīkshitar This only shows that in spite of the royal command there remained a good deal more to be done by way of conciliating the śaivite scholars before actually giving effect to the order and this also points to the fact that Chidambaram must have already become a stronghold of Śaivism.

There is no inscription to indicate that in Achyuta's time or prior to that there was a separate shrine for Govindarāja Achyuta did not build any for the Visnu deity Prior to the time of Kulōttunga II, Natarāja and Govindarāja must have been installed in the same place and Kulōttunga II must have removed the image of Govindarāja (Mulavar) to one of the Tirumaligaipattis (platforms). It was several years after Achyuta's death (i e. 1599 A D) important constructions were made in Visnu shrine The

---

1 V A Smith's Oxford History of India p 305

setting up of a separate worship according to Vaikhānasa form in the Viṣṇu shrine therefore indicates that the deity must have existed before in some place or other in the vicinity of Natarāja. Otherwise it is inconceivable why a patchwork should have been made in Vijayanagar days of breaking up an old Chōla wall for effecting a new and separate entrance to Govindarāja shrine and constructing vimana thereon and building other walls that were not quite in keeping with the symmetry of the other parts of the temple. After Kulōttunga II there must have been a reaction in favour of the Viṣṇu shrine and the shrine was allowed to continue in some form or other and this accounts for the tradition ascribed to Vēdānta Dēśika that he consecrated the idol long before the Vijayanagar kings took the idea into their head

Passing on to the Vijayanagar period, an epigraph on a slab in the Pasupatīśvara temple at Tiruvētkalam records the grant of that village to the Chidambaram temple by Achyutappa Nāyaka, son of Siṟu-śevappa Nāyaka for the merit of Tirumalairājayaṉ (*i.e.* the Karnatá king, Tirumala I. Tirumala was a staunch Vaiṣṇava and is credited with having made the tūlapurusa and other gifts at important shrines including Chidambaram.

The next inscriptions[1] of interest in the Chidambaram temple are those of the Vijayanagar kings—Vēṅkata I (1586-1614) and Ranga III (1642-1680) and one of their chiefs *viz.* Vaiyappa-Kríshnappa-Koṇḍama Nāyakkar, who is frequently

---

1 A R. E 348, 359, 369 of 1913.

mentioned in these inscriptions, presented several villages to the temple and also declared tax-free all the villages owned by the temple from early times. Muthukrishṇappa Nāyaka, son of Koṇḍama Nāyaka is said to have made some repairs to the temple during the time of Vēṅkata I.

There is an interesting account of a contemporary observer[1] to show that considerable improvements were made to this shrine about 1599 A.D. Krishṇappa Nāyaka of Gingee was about this time in Chidambaram superintending the improvements and the construction of the Dvajasthamba. The Dīkśhitars protested against the Nāyak's improvements in the Viṣṇu temple and some of them even killed themselves by falling

1. Sources of Vijayanagar History–Edited by S. Krisnaswami Iyengar p. 272.

Father N Pimenta who passed through Chidambaram in 1597 and was an eye-witness to certain incidents that took place there when Krishnappa Nāyaka made certain improvements, says that a great controversy arose as to "whether it was lawful to place the signe of Perimal (which is nothing but a Mast or Pole gilded with an Ape at the foot) in the temple at Chidambaram. Some refused; others by their Legats importunately urged and the Naichus of Gingi decreed to erect it in the temple" But when Krishnappa carried out the reconstruction and repair of the temple in spite of the opposition, the priests of the Siva temple climbed the tower "and cast themselves down", while he was in the temple and thus twenty of them died. Krishnappa got angry and ordered the rest to be shot which order was obeyed and two were so done away with. "A woman also was so hote in this zealous quarrel that she cut her own throat." (Purchas. His Pilgrims, pp 208-209)

from the top of the tower. Krishṇappa Nāyaka is said to have accomplished his purpose in spite of opposition. Probably the structures which were renovated during the time of the Vijayanagara king were consecrated during the time of the famous Krishṇappa Nāyaka of Gingee.

The inscription relating to the reign of Ranga III which takes us to the middle of the 17th century A D. is of particular interest.[1] It is Saka 1565 (*i.e.* A.D. 1643) and records that the king repaired the big Mandapa in front of the Tillai Govindarājaswāmi shrine, the gōpura of the shrine, the Vimanas of the Goddesses Puṇḍarīkavalli Nāchiyār and Sūḍikoḍutta Nāchiyār and the Mandapa in front of the shrine of Tiruvāḷi Ālvān.

VIII

We may next sketch briefly the vicissitudes of the temple in the Carnatic wars of the 18th century. The temple was used as a fort first in 1760 and later in 1780[2] The French took Chidambaram in 1753 and held it during the war till 1760. During these years the French began a series of fortifications about the temple consisting of four batteries from the four corners of the outermost of the stone walls which enclose the temple and another battery in the centre of each of the two longer (eastern and western) sides of this wall. The French garrison which occupied Chidambaram surrendered to Major Monson on 12th April 1760.

1. A. R. E. 271 of 1913
2. Cambridge · War in India, p. 131; Orme's History Vol. III (4th Edition) gives the plan.

In 1760 Colonel Coote after defeating Lally at Wandiwash and driving him back into Pondichery possessed himself without much trouble of Cuddalore and Chidambaram previously to taking Pondichery which fell in January 1761.

During the invasion of the Carnatic by Haidar Ali of Mysore in 1780, some of his troops occupied Chidambaram and the temple. In 1781 Coote was defeated in a night attack on the fortified pagoda then garrisoned by Haidar. The attacking party under Coote's personal direction were repulsed with considerable loss after forcing their way through two of the three enclosures of the western gateway of the temple.[1] It was during this disturbed period that Naṭarāja was removed from

---

1. "Eyre Coote marched against the place and sent three battalions to clear the enemy out of the town After a scattered fire the latter took refuge in the temple and by some mistake and without orders, the foremost of the English battalions pursued them up to its gateway—apparently that under the western tower Finding this shut, they brought up *a twelve-pounder to burst it open* and the second shot from this broke down the outer of the two gates under the tower The sponge-staff had however been fired out of the gun in the hurry and the man who carried the match was not to be found Captain Moorhouse of the Artillery nevertheless loaded and discharged the gun twice by means of a musket and made a breach in the inner gate *large enough, to let through one man at a time* The sepoys *rushed into* the space between the two gateways which in a moment was full of them, but did not observe midway between the two a flight of steps which led to a rampart The garrison every moment dreading the general assault called for quarter but their cries could not be distinguished in the general tumult.

his shrine by the Dīkśhitars and taken over to Tiruvārūr (in the Tanjore district) for safety. An inscription in grantha character in the form of a 'slōka' in the 1000 pillared 'maṇḍapa' refers to this fact and says that it was in the year Saka 1695 Kali 4874 (in the month of Māsi, Kriśṇapaksha mūla nakshatra trayōdasi tithi) that Naṭarāja came back to Chit Sabhā from Tiruvārūr.

During the close of the 18th century, a *paruana* of the Nawab of Arcot shows that the shrine of Govindarāja had to be closed owing to disputes and worship was commenced after the intervention of the Nawab The Dīkśhitars admit in the said *paruanu* that they had beaten the servants and soldiers posted at the door of the shrine for continuing the worship The Dīkśhitars also admit that they had intended to pull down the Visṇu temple—an object which was partly accomplished when the Ardha Maṇḍapam was suddenly pulled during the renovation of the temple by the Nāṭṭukōttai Chettiars

Meanwhile some straw became ignited and set fire to the clothes of the sepoys who were crowded between the gateways and every one pressing back to avoid suffocation and the fire of the enemy (which was redoubled at the sight of this mishap) many of them were scorched and burnt to death, and those who escaped hurried officers away without attempting to bring the twelve-pounder Six officers and nearly 150 men were killed or wounded in this unfortunate affair The General who was in the pettah at the time ordered some pieces of cannon to batter the wall A fine brass 18 pounder was ruined without making any breach and then, as day was beginning to dawn, the troops returned to camp All thoughts were now abandoned of taking the place by assault (District Gazetter pp 266-67)

The history of the temple in the 19th century is only remarkable for the constant litigation between the trustees of the two shrines of Naṭarāja and Govindaraja. There is no record of the construction or reconstruction of any portion of the temple since the 16th century until we come to the period of renovation by Nāṭṭukkōṭṭai Chettiars in recent times in pursuance of an agreement between the Dīkshitars and the Chettiars towards the close of the 19th century.

CHAPTER V

ARCHITECTURE.

The purpose of temple art and architecture was to glorify religion by telling its story in most expressive form which the chisel of the sculptor could command. When we make all allowance for the destruction wrought by time and man, it must be recognised that during the mediaeval period Hinduism commanded the best that India could give not only in money, but also in taste and skill. The mediaeval period of South Indian history was a great age of temple building. The Pallavas are still remembered by the temple at Conjeevaram, and the great days of the Chōlas by that at Tanjore. Some western critics object to the quantity and elaboration of ornament in some of the religious edifices of South India on the ground that they tend to obscure the fundamental qualities of the edifice, but all of them recognise that the union of strength and grace displayed in some of the best temple structures is unsurpassed.

The Chidambaram temple which belongs to the mediaeval age of temple building exhibits some of the charateristics of Dravidian architecture. Most of the structures range from the 10th to the 16th century A. D. The Chidambaram temple was not built in its entirety like the great temple at Tanjore. It has 'grown by accident rather than design.' Its various edifices are not parts of any general scheme, and yet the general effect of the architecture of the temple is very striking. The age of the oldest part of the temple is not easy to dogmatise but from the architectural point of view, according to Fergusson, no part of the temple is much older than the 10th century.

The Chit Sabhā. It is the central shrine of the temple and is a plain wooden building standing on a stone basement. The roof of the Chitsabhā is covered with plates of gold.

The Kanakasabhā. It is a small porch in front of the Chit Sabhā standing on a stone basement with wooden doors all round. It is roofed with plates of copper

The Vishnu Shrine Almost adjoining the Chit Sabhā and the Kanakasabhā is the shrine of Govindaraja. The style of architecture employed in constructing this shrine belongs to the Vijayanagar period. A portion of the *Tirumalaipatti* of the Naṭarāja shrine was used for building the Garbhagraha of Govindarāja. A Chōla wall was cut through in several places for inserting the Vijayanagar wall of Govindarāja shrine. The stones of the Govindarāja shrine were not so finely dressed and smooth as the stones of the original Chōla walls. The entire shrine of Govindarāja has been renovated recently so that there are few traces of the old style.

The Nritta Sabhā, or the 'hall of the dance.' It is the most beautiful and the most interesting part of the temple from an architectural point of view. It consists of a mantapā adorned with wheels and prancing horses on either side to represent a celestial vehicle. It is supported by

56 pillars about 8 ft. high and most delicately carved, from top to bottom resting on a stylobate ornamented with dancing figures which Fergusson describes as being 'more graceful and more eloquently executed than any others of their class in Southern India' He says that 'white wash and modern alterations have sadly disfigured this gem, but enough remains to show how exquisite and consequently how ancient it was.' The famous dance of Siva in which he raised one of his legs above his head is represented within the Nritta Sabhâ by one of the finest dancing icons of Naṭarāja.

Amman shrine. According to Fergusson this shrine "is principally remarkable for its porch, which is of singular elegance. The outer aisles are 6 feet in width but the architect reserved all his power for the central aisle which measures 21 feet 6 inches in width making the whole 50 feet or thereabout. In order to roof this without employing stones of such dimensions as would crush the supports, recourse was had to vaulting or rather bracketing shafts and these brackets were again tied together by tranverse purlins, all in stone and the system was continued till the width was reduced to a dimension that could easily be spanned. As the whole is enclosed in a court surrounded by galleries two storeys in height, the effect of the whole is singularly pleasing."

From the top of one of the pillars of the aisle hangs a chain of several movable links cut from one piece of stone. In a corner of the court is one of several wells in the temple which are lined with circular rings of stone about 4 feet in outside diameter, each cut from a single slab

The Pāndyanāyaka shrine It is a portico of square pillars four in front, and all most elaborately ornamented The design of the pillars resembles that of the piers in the Nritta sabhā All round the stone basement of the shrine are to be found the most delicately carved, fine dancing poses This shrine is in the form of a mandapa with wheels, prancing horses and elephants on either side to represent a celestial vehicle The age of this shrine is difficult to decide but according to the character of its ornamentation and its position, according to Fergussion it belongs to the end of the 17th and first half of the 18th century But from its style, it should be given an earlier date

The 1000 pillared mandapa It is some 340 feet by 180 feet and is more modern than most of the buildings. It is one of the five sabhās or halls of the temple and is called Rājasabha or hall of state In the words of Fergusson, "the pillars are arranged in twenty four in front by forty one in depth making 984, but in order to get a central space, four in the porch, then twenty eight, then two, and again twenty-four have been omitted, altogether fifty eight, but on the other hand, those of the external portico must be added, which nearly balances the loss, and makes up the 1000 It must be confessed that this forest of granite pillars, each of a single stone and all more or less carved and ornamented does produce a certain grandeur of effect, but the want of design in the arrangement and of subordination of parts, detract painfully from the effect that might have been produced. Leaving out the pillars in the centre is the one redeeming feature, and that could easily have been effected without the brick vaults, formed of radiating arches which are employed here—a certain proof of the modern age of the building. These vaults are certainly integral, as certainly could not have been employed till after the Muhammadans had settled in the south, and taught the Hindus how to use them. "This huge hallw as possibly erected between 1595 and 1685 at which time, we learn from the Mackenzie Mss the kings of the locality made many donations to the fane."

The gōpuras. There are four gōpuras facing the four points of the compass. The lower part of each gōpura, is, as usual, of stone, and the upper, of brick and mortar richly decorated with plaster figures painted in colours. The northern gōpura which was begun in the days of Krishnadēvaraya is about 157 feet above sea level and is 140 feet above ground In the inner wall of the northern gōpura there are stone sculptured figures one of which is identified as Krishnadēva and above these sculptured figures, we find in characters of the 16th century the names of four figures by name (1) Viruddhagiriyil Sēvakkappermāl; (2) his son Viśvamuttu (3) Tiruppiraikkodai Āchāri Tirumaruṅgam and (4) his brother Kārañ Āchari. The eastern gōpura seems (from inscriptional record) to have been built sometime in the 13th century by Kōpperuñjiṅgadēvā and renovated later by Pachaiyappa Mudaliar of Conjeevaram On the lower stone portions of the gōpura the decoration for the most part consists of little panels containing dancing figures which are connected with the central idea of the Naṭarāja temple—the mystic dance of Śiva and they form a predominant feature in the architecture of the temple.

The west gōpura must have also been built about the 13th century as is evidenced by the literary references and inscriptional record. The niches containing images of deities in the east wall of the west gōpura[1] give in the characters of the 13th century A. D., the names of the images which are as follows: Kāmadēvan, Agasthyan̲, Sridēvi, Dēvēndran̲, Gaṇēśvarar and Durggādēvi. The images in niches in the north wall of the west gōpura[2] are Rudhradēvar, Rāhu Kēthukkaḷ, Nāradan̲ Aḷakēśvaran̲, Chandhran̲, Kriyāsakti, Śan̲ibhagavān̲ and Vāyubhagavān̲. The niches in the west wall of the west gōpura[3] contain the images of Kshētrapāla Piḷḷayār, Gaṅgadēvi, Dhanvantari (Tripura) Sundaridevi, Sukran̲, Vaijayan̲, Nāga, Yamunai, Bhadrakāḷi and Ādichaṇḍēśvarar. In the south wall of the west gōpura, the niches contain the images of Niruti; Budhan̲, Gñān̲aśakti and Agn̲idēvan̲.

The southern gōpura must have been undertaken by a Pāṇḍya king as is evidenced by the crest of the fish in the central cross stone of the gateway of the gōpura and its completion in the form of a superstructure with seven storeys is mentioned in the Āttūr incription of Kōpperuñjiṅgadēva.

1. A. R. E. 21-26 of 1936.
2. A R E. 27-34 of 1936.
3. A. R. E. 35-44 of 1936.

The two inner enclosures of the temple which were originally built during the mediaeval Chōla period have in recent years been renovated and added to by the Nāṭṭukkōṭṭai Chettiars. The most striking part of the new additions is a great covered cloister of imposing width in the second enclosure. The cloister is roofed with stone slabs supported on long rows of tall covered granite pillars, some 25 feet high and all of the same design. The carving is good and the general effect is striking.

We may conclude this brief sketch of temple architecture with a few general observations. With the coming of the Chōlas the temple emerges as an architecturally important and monumental structure in stone. The royal builders seem to have outdone their predecessors. The urge for bigness which characterises the temple structure of the mediaeval period was the result of many influences upon the Indian mind and it was intensified probably by the ideals of a prosperous and powerful age. The organisation of the resources under energetic rulers made such temple building possible. It was an age in which the public was trained to expect and appreciate bigness, efficient organization of labour and the manifestation of power and wealth. The rulers built large temples not only because they enjoyed them aesthetically but they also considered them necessary and useful. Temples propitiated the gods and were also eternal evidence of the devotion of the royal builders. Each successive king, if he had the resources and initiative, was inclined to build new ones or enlarge the old and carve his name and attainments on the walls of the temple. Hence many of the temples of South India are the result of successive additions whereby each king sought to out-do the greatness of his ancestors The result is that a few of the big temples like the Chidambaram temple appear to be lacking in any unified sense of design, but in spite of their apparent diversity, the actual elements and their arrangement followed rigid conventions The basic parts of the temple were always along traditional lines. No matter how large and complicated a temple might be, it consisted of a multiplication of the essential parts and the extension of the parts in length was both a natural method of building and the result of the ritual which required a corridor-like plan because of its pre occupation with processions Like palaces which were the private retreat of the high ruler, the temples were often placed within a sacred enclosure surrounded by high and protective walls

Some of the big temples of South India are standing monuments of the achievements of Dravidian architecture The super-human size still connotes greatness, power and magnificence It is not necessary to ask if these structures are beautiful or if their sheer bulk reflect a drying up of Indian imagination They are undoubtedly grandiose and since they represent the greatest material effort of mediaeval rulers to mould stone to their desires, they deserve respect and study

CHAPTER VI

SCULPTURE

The sculptures from Hindu temples are the most authentic examples and illustration of Hindu mythology Some of the finest and most interesting sculptures of the Chidambaram temple are found in the gōpuras, the Nritta Sabhā, the Pāndyanāyakam, the Tirumaligaipāti of Śivakāmi Sundari shrine. The outer walls of the gōpuras contain images enshrined in niches. We may refer to some of them which are most interesting from the iconographic point of view.

1. *Brahma* According to Mānasāra one of the standard works on sculpture, Brahma is represented with four heads He has, however only one body and four hands The image may be standing or seated Images of Brahma are commonly found on one of the niches in the north wall of the central shrine in a Śiva temple Images of Brahma may also be seen on pillars or other parts of a temple The image of Brahma riding on a swan in a niche on the west side of the east gōpura of the Natarāja temple is interesting The illustration in the temple shows Brahma on his swan vehicle folding two of his hands, in a worshipping posture and holding the rosary (akasbamala) and water pot (kamandalu) in the other two. He has (i) ear-rings or pendants fashioned like the face of a crocodile (ii) the sacred thread (yajñasūtra) hanging right accross the body from above the left shoulder (iii) the necklace (iv) armlets, wristlets, anklets etc His head has the

jatāmakuṭa This stone image of Brahma in the Chidambaram temple is interesting as it is rarely that the swan vehicle is found in the figures of Brahma set up in South Indian temples.

2. *Garuda Nārāyana*. The silpasāra mentions an image called Garuda Nārāyana in which Visnu is seen riding on Garuda holding a bow and discus The stone images of Visnu riding on the bird Garuda are found in niches on the west side of the east gōpura, and on the east side of the west gōpura While these images are somewhat mutilated, there is a fine image of Garuda Nārāyana in the south side of the north gōpura.

3 *Patañjali* The image of Patañjali usually accompanies the image of Natarāja. The Tanjore inscriptions (S. I. I. Vol. II Introduction) describe the image of Patañjali as "three quarters and one-eighth (of a muham) in height from the tail to the hoods (*Phana*). It has five hoods, one face in the midst of these hoods, one crown (*makuta*), two divine arms above the navel, a human body and below the navel, three coils. This description closely agrees with the figure of Patañjali in a niche on the north side of the east gōpura. (Fig 2)

4 *Vyāghrapāda*. In a niche on the south side of the east gōpura is a stone image of Vyāghrapāda in which the sage is represented as having tiger's claws on both his hands and feet The sage is carrying on his right shoulder a hook and a flower basket. (Fig 3).

5 *Vinādhara—Dakshināmūrti*. The Āgamās mention 25 sportive forms (līla-murtis) of Śiva

most of which are usually found in South Indian temples. One of the more important is Dakshinā-mūrthi. When Dakshinamūrthi holds in his fore-arms the lute *vīna* and changes the posture of his left leg apparently for keeping the vīna in position, he is called Vināḍhara-Dakshināmūrthi The bull vehicle of the god is also seen in the figure in the Chidambaram temple.

6 *Lingōdbhva*, 'the manifestation of Śiva' is seen on the west wall of the central shrine of Śiva temples There is an image of Lingōdbhava in a shrine on the west side of the Chit sabha surrounded by flames of fire Lingodbhava as the name implies is represented within a huge linga, the portions of the feet below the ankles being hidden in the linga. The story is that a dispute arose between Brahma and Visnu as to who is the greater of the two. Śiva told them that whoever first saw the top or the bottom of his own fiery linga form and came back to report would be the greater of the two Brahma soared on his swan to see the top of the Śivalinga while Visnu as a boar dug down and down to see its bottom Ages passed and neither came to his goal At last Brahma came back and uttered a lie saying he had seen the top of the linga and this roused the wrath of Śiva who cursed him

7 *Kalyānasundara* Siva decorated as bride-groom is called Kalyānasundara In this form he is represented as a fair youth On his side stands Parvati as bride whose right hand he holds with his own The general posture of the god is what is called samabhanga and the left leg firmly placed

on the ground. A fine representation of Kalyānasundara and Svayamvara is found on the west side of the eastern gōpura. (Fig 4)

8 *Kiratārjunamūrti.* A form of Śiva in which he is supposed to have appeared before Arjuna when the latter was doing penance to obtain from Śiva a powerful weapon (Pāsupata) with which he could destroy his enemies. In the illustration that is found at the Chidambaram temple in a niche on the north side of the east gōpura Śiva as Kritarjunamūrti wears both the arrow and the bow. There is also a figure of Arjuna in a worshipping posture

9 *Tripurantakamūrti.* Śiva assumed this form when he killed the three demons called Tripura and reduced their cities to ashes The Earth is said to have served as a chariot and the Sun and the Moon as its wheels The four Vedas were the four horses and the Upanishads were the guiding reins The mountain Meru was the bow, the ocean was the quiver, and god Visnu was the arrow Images of Tripurantaka are made with the right leg firmly placed on the pedestal and the left leg bent The right forehand holds the arrow, the left forearm the bow, the other hands hold the tanka (or the axe) and the deer respectively The locks are arranged in the form of a jatamakuta and the goddess Gauri stands on the left side The image of Śiva as Tripurantakamūrti in the Chidambaram temple answers to this description (Fig 5)

10. *Chandeśānugrahamūrti* A form of Siva which was assumed by him in order to confer blessings on his fervent devotee Chandēśa, his figure is occasionally found depicted in some of

the South Indian temples. On the east gōpura of the temple is a figure of Chandēśānugrahamurti in which Chandēsa is represented with the axe between his folded arms. There is another stone image of Chaṇḍēśānugrahamūrti on the west side of the southern gōpura.

11. *Pasupātamūrti*, is a fierce form of Śiva. For purposes of meditation, a milder form is adopted in which like Chandrasēkhara the god is represented standing or seated with a smiling countenance showing the trident and the abhaya in his two right arms, the rosary and the varada in the two left arms. (Fig. 6)

12. *Sūrya* In a niche on the east side of the north gōpura is a fine stone image of Sūrya. He is represented as composed of Brahma Mahēśvara and Visnu On the pedestal are shown seven horses driven by Aruṇa who, though believed to be without legs, is here represented with them

13. *Indra.* A Vēdic god. In a niche on the eastern side of the east gōpura, there is a stone image of Indra riding on the celestial elephant Airāvata. The front two hands are in the abhaya and varada poses and the back hands carry the ankusa and the vajra (Fig. 7)

14. *Agni*; the most prominent of the Vēdic gods Agni as an image is generally represented to be an old man, the oldest of the gods and a counterpart of Sun on earth. He has a red body, two heads and six eyes and seven arms. He is surrounded by a circle of light His vehicle is the

ram and his banner, the smoke issuing from the sacrificial fire-pit. There is a stone image of Agni in a niche on the south side of the east gōpura. In his seven arms he holds the vessels prōkshani (sprinkles), srik (ladle), sruva (spoon), pūrṇa-pātra (vessel full of water), tomara (pestle), fan, and the ghee pot required in performing a sacrifice. A bull (not a ram as required by the Āgamas) is sculptured behind Agni as his vehicle.

15. *Yama*—the god of death He usually exhibits the club, noose, abhaya and varada in his *four arms and rides on a buffalo In a niche contain*ing a stone image of Yama on the south side of the east gōpura, the figures shows only two hands in which are held the gada (club) and the pasa (noose). There is a small Karandamakuṭa on the head and a number of ornaments on the person. His vehicle, a buffalo, is standing behind him.

16. *Ādiśēsha*. In a niche containing a stone image of Ādiśēsha in the east gōpura, Ādiśesha is represented in a semi-human form. (Fig. 8).

17. *Narada.* Saints and sages are figured in temples. They are seated in a meditative posture with the rosary or a book and the waterpot or staff in their hands. The sacred thread, braided hair, flowing beards and moustaches form the special features of rishi images. In a niche containing the stone image of Narada in the east gōpura of the temple, Narada as usual is distinguished from other sages by the Vīṇa which he holds in his hands. (Fig. 9)

18 *Agastya.* The stone image of Agastya in a niche on the east gōpura of the temple represents him as dwarfish in stature and pot-bellied. According to tradition Agastya is supposed to have migrated from the north to the south and to have dwelt there permanently and developed the Tamil language of which he is said to be the first grammarian.

19 *Kaṅkalamūrti.* The image of Kaṅkalamūrti is generally found in almost all Śiva temples of importance in southern India The figures of Kaṅkalamūrti, one on the southern side of the northern gōpura and another on the western side of the eastern gōpura of the Chidambaram temple conform closely to the description given in Śaivāgamās. The figure is a standing one with the left leg planted firmly on the ground and the right slightly bent and kept a bit forward suggesting that the figure is in the act of moving. The head is ornamented with the Jaṭamakuta. There is a snake on the right side with the crescent moon. The ears are adorned with Kuṇdalas. Of the four hands, the front right one keeps the bāna i.e. a short resined stick used in exciting the membrane of a sort of drum known by the name of dhakka. The back right arm is stretched out and its hand held in the kaṭaka pose near the mouth of his pet animal, the deer, and in the back left hand, there is the Kaṅkāla-danda or the staff on which the bones and legs are tied up together. This Kaṅkāla-danda is placed horizontally on the left shoulder., one end being held by the back left hand The mūrti wears a pair of sandals on his feet and is surrounded by a

number of bhūtagaṇas, rishis, devas etc, with arms crossed on the chest in the anjali pose

20 *Tarakari Subramanya* The fine stone image of Subramanya in the east side of the western gōpura is riding on a pecock and spiritedly attacking the giants evidently-Tarakasura and his retinue There are three visible faces and ten arms In four of his right hands he holds the weapons, sword, axe, arrow and club, while the fifth is on the posture of pulling the bow string. The uppermost of his left arms shows the vismaya posture and the four others hold the shield, bow, noose and bell On either side of Subrahmanya are the Devas in the alidhasana posture flying in the air and praising him

21 *Vrishavāhana* Śiva in a standing posture leaning against his vahana the bull, is called Vrishavāhana The elbow (Kurpura) of the right hand of Śiva rests on the head of the bull A fine image of Vrishavahanamurti is found in a niche on the west side of the eastern gōpura of the temple

The East and West gōpuras of the temple are rich in sculptures whose artistic value is increased by the explanatory labels attached to most of them The inner walls of the gōpuras contain the well-known figures representing the sculptural exposition of the art of dancing The images representing dancing postures with descriptive verses are found in the eastern gōpura of the temple Though the dance poses are found all over the temple, the dancing figures in relief in the Nritta sabha, the Pandyanāyakam, the Tirumalapati of Śivakamasundari shrine are most ancient structures and are most exquisitely carved. Some of the most graceful poses most elegantly executed in the stylobate of the Nṛitta sabha are reproduced here. The Annual Report of Epigraphy (1914) gives a reproduction of the dancing figures with descriptive verses found in the eastern gōpura of the temple and the patron of these decorative structures was Kopperunjiṅga, who built the eastern gōpura of the temple.

The glory of the Chidambaram temple lies in the fact that it exemplifies one of the important dancing postures of Śiva–the dance of bliss (Aṅanda tāndavam.[1] There are many references in early Tamil literature to the dance of Śiva at Chidambaram. Such expressions as செம்பொன்னினில் எழுதி வேய்ந்த சிற்றம்பல கூத்தனை, தில்லையம்பலக்கூத்தனை, தில்லையம்பலத்தாடுகின்ற அத்தரவுள்ளுடல் of Appar and பொன்னம்பலக்கூத்தா of Māṇikkavāśagar serve to indicate the sacredness of the temple, as the place of Śiva's Dance, but the Dēvāram hymners do not specify the name of the deity.

There are many dances of Siva. The fundamental idea underlying all these dances is more or less the same *viz.* the outward expression of primal rhythmic energy. The origin of Śiva's dance is a most interesting but baffling inquiry. Whatever the origins of Śiva's Dancé, it became in time the clearest image of the activity of God. It is not

---

1. "The Lord of Tillai's Court, a mystic dance performs, what is that, my dear? (Tiruvāchagam—Pope's edition)

possible to interpret here the various dances of Śiva. Some of the well-known dances of Śiva are the evening dance, the Tāndava and the Nadanta Dance of Natarāja.

The evening dance in the Kailas is described in the Śiva Pratōsha Ślōtra In the evening dance, Śiva is only two handed and the co-operation of the gods is implied in their position of chorus. There is no prostrate Asura under Śiva's feet. One should like to know whether there is any special interpretation of this dance in Saiva literature

Another well-known dance of Śiva is called the Tāndava It belongs to his *tamasic* aspect as Bhairava and it is in the burning grounds that Śiva performs this dance with Devi The Tāndava Dance is in origin that of a pre-Āryan deity afterwards merged in Śiva An interpretation of this dance is given in Śaiva and Sakta literature

The next and most important dance for us in the dance of bliss (Ānanta-Tāndavam) of Natarāja in the golden hall of Tillai and this dance was performed by Śiva to gods and the rishis,–Vyaghrapāda and Patañjali,—who were performing penance in Tillai in order to enjoy the beatific sight of Śiva's Dance. Śiva is best known as the Dancer. His Dance is Evolution, Continuance and Involution Nataraja is a form of Śiva and the word means 'Lord of the Dance' Śiva as Nataraja has four arms, he has braided locks and these locks whirl in the dance. On the head are cobra in a twisted form, a mermaid figure of the Ganges and the crescent moon He has a man's ear ring in the right ear, and a woman's in the left. One hand holds a drum sounding the call to all the people who are immersed in 'samsāra to go to him for protection, another hand holds fire to give assurance of help to his devotees; of the other two hands, one is raised (abhayamudra) 'do not fear' and the other points to the lifted foot (Kuñjitapāda) which confers mōksha or eternal bliss on all worshippers. Beneath the right leg, there lies the dwarf Muyalakan. The concept of Naṭarāja is the synthesis of a long evolution. There are 108 postures of dancing according to the Bhārata Nāṭṭya Śāstra. The postures recommended in dancing to please the daityas are numberless and a selected list of 108 of them called Karanas or single postures and 32 selected Angahāras (combinations of two or more of these Karanas) are fully described. As has already been pointed out, in the east gōpura of the Naṭarāja temple, these karanas are found cut on stones with appropriate verses from the Nāṭṭya sāstra underneath each of the postures. Only 93 of these postures were recovered, the remaining 15 were either damaged or the compartments of the gōpura altered during the repairs done to the temple. These postures are found in Bharata's order for about 60 numbers and then owing to mason's or supervisor's ignorance or on account of some subsequent alteration in the construction, the remaining 48 are not in the order followed by Bharata. These sculptures are published in the Report on Epigraphy (1914). Similar dance poses are also found in the inner sides of the southern and western gōpuras

Missing Page

conception itself as a synthesis of science, religion and art. How amazing the range of thought and sympathy of those rishi-artists who first conceived such a type as this, affording an image of reality a key to the complex tissue of life, a theory of nature not satisfactory to a single clique or race, nor acceptable to the thinkers of one contry only, but u niversal in its appeal to the Philosopher, the Bhakta, and the artist of all ages and all countries. No artist of to-day, however great, could more exactly or more wisely create an image of that energy which science must postulate behind all phenomena If we could reconcile Time with Eternity, we can scarcely do so otherwise than by the conception of alterations of phase extending over vast regions of space and great tracts of time. Especially significant then is the phase of alteration implied by the drum and the fire which 'changes', not destroys. These are but visual symbols of the theory of the day and night of Brahma.

Naṭarāja is not only Truth but Love; for the purpose of His Dance is Grace, the giving of freedom to countless individual souls. Lastly also how supremely great in power and grace this dancing image must appear to all those who as artists have striven in plastic forms to give expression to their intuition of Life It is not strange that the figure of Naṭarāja has commanded the adoration of so many generations past; we, familiar with all scepticisms, expert in tracing all beliefs to primitive superstitions, explorers of the infinitely great and infinitely small, are worshippers of Sri Naṭarāja still."

APPENDIX I

CLASSIFIED LIST OF INSCRIPTIONS IN THE CHIDAMBARAM TEMPLE

CHŌLA KINGS

PARAKĒSARI RĀJĒNDRA I

This is the earliest record in the temple The praśasti is not in the usual form Gift of
Year 24
viravunilan elupattettekālē—eraikkāni; deducting land taken up by .ōḍai nāraikālāṟu, kollai;and nattam, making up muppattu-nālēkālē-araikkāni, the net arable land was forty vēli The total yield was 4,500 kalam of paddy, of this the melvāram was 2,250 kalam which yielded 264¾ kāśu which with 40 kāśu from another source formed the fund for the expenses in-the temple. (118 of 1888) [For text, *vide* S I I. Vol. IV—No 223 Ed by H Krishna Sastri]

KULŌTTUNGA I

Records several gifts to the god (Aluḍaiyār) of Chidambaram (Tillai or Tiruchirrambalam)
Year 44
by Rājarājan-Kundavai, the younger sister of Tribhuvanachakravartin Kulōttunga Sōradeva. Further it records that Rājēndra Sōra-deva put up at the temple in the front row of 'edirambalam' a stone which he had *received from the King of Kāmboja*. A portion of the inscription was published in Indian Antiquary Vol. XXIII, p 298 and Epigraphica Indica Vol IV pp 70 and also Epigraphica Indica Vol. V, p 105 Rajaraja Kundavai-Alvar gave a gold vessel (fifty kalañju of the fine-

ness of madhurāntakam (mādai) for tannir-amudu to Āḷudaiyār. A Tamil verse states that in year 44 of Jayadhara (Friday 13th March A.D. 1114—Epigraphica Indica Vol. IV pp. 71-72) the same lady covered with gold the whole of the temple, 'tillaināyakar-tan-kōyilelānisembonmēyndāl.' She also gave a mirror (tirukkannādi) to the nāyaka-dēva (119 of 1888).

Year 46 Refers to the purchase of a dēvadāna by a private individual (291 of 1913). Unfinished.

Year 46 and 160th day Mentions Madurāntaki, 'the younger sister of our lord.' Sirrambalam is here also called Puliyur. Land by Madurāntaki for a flower-garden and for feeding Māheśvaras (117 of 1888); also S. I. I. Vol. IV—222.

Year 47 This is stated to be *a copy of an inscription originally engraved on the opposite "Edir Ambalam"* (shrine); gift of land by purchase for supplying garlands of red lotuses to the temple (290 of 1913).

Not dated Two Sanskrit verses which praise the victories of Kūlōttunga-Chōla over the five Pandyas and the Keralas, and which record that he burnt the fort of Korgara and that he put up a pillar of victory on a peak of the Sahyadri mountains (115 of 1888, also S.I.I. Vol. I, 155, E. I. Vol. V, pp. 103-4).

Not dated *Sanskrit fragment (116 of 1888).*

Not dated Records in Tamil in nine fragmentary stones. One of the fragments mentions the name of the king Tribhuvana Chakravartin Kulōttunga chōla deva. Two others contain part of the historical introduction of Kulottunga Chola I, and the rest provide offerings to the temple (545 of 1916)

VIKRAMA CHŌLA

Year 3 and 95th day — Records gift of land by a native of Tiraimūr in Tiraimunādu which was a district of Uyyokondan-valanādu at Manārkudi a hamlet of Jayankonda sōla chaturvedimangalam in Merkal nadu, a sub division of Virudarājabhauan karavalanādu, for a flower-garden Also records another gift of land in Pannangudichcheri alias Parakesarinallur which has a hamlet of Perumbarrapuliyūr with four tenants (kudi) for maintaining the garden and for providing the mantrapushpa in the temple of Tiruchirrambalam-Udaiyār (268 of 1913).

Year 5 and 351st day — Registers gift of 116 velis of land of Adur alias Jananāthanallūr to 108 Brahmanas, to the god Ulagamuladudaiya-Pillayar, the matha etc, of Ulagamuladudaiyachaturvedimangalam a hamlet on the western side of Perumbarrapuliyur The recipient had to measure out four kalams on each veli of land to the temple of Tillainayaka as the donees of Vikramapandya chaturvedimangalam did–(278 of 1913)

Year 8 — Mentions Nangur in Nangur-nādu, contains a portion of the historical introduction of Rajaraja I (A D 985–1013) –(551 of 1918)

Not dated — It is a long defaced inscription in Sanskrit and Tamil Records the achievements of Naralokavira, one of the royal chieftains (For Text *vide* S I. I. Vol IV—Texts Ed by H. Krishna Sastri No 225)—(120 of 1888)

KULOTTUNGA III

Year 2 and 121st day Refers the order registered in Inscription No. 262 and says it was issued by Villavarayan at the request of Vaidumbarayan. The document is signed by ten officers of the king of whom the Tirumandira-olai-nāyaka was Narayana Muvendavelan (263 of 1913)

Year 2 and 125th day Registers an order of the king that from that date the assessed lands (taram-perra-nilam) standing in the name of the Subrahmanya-Piḷḷaiyar shrine in the Arumoḷisvara temple of the village be included with those of the latter, that lands declared to be superior to the eighth class be assessed as per those of the eighth class (eṭṭām-taram) and that those below the eighth class be allowed to continue as before, and that the site of the temple of Tiruttoṇḍattogai-Īśvaram-Udaiyar, its enclosures, premises and the sacred tank etc., till now included in the account of assessed lands be removed from that register. The order was executed by the Land Survey Committee (niḷam-aḷavupadapperumakkal) of the village assemly of Perumbarrappuliyūr. Full details of the extent, boundaries etc. of the land are given. (262 of 1913).

Year 3 Records that under orders of Toṇḍaiman a land presented at Midimikkuḍi alias Dāna-vinōdanallūr for a flower garden was made tax-free and the same was engraved on the walls of Vikramaśoḷan-tirumāligai.

Year 5 Mentions Nandipaoman. For text, *vide* S. I. I. Vol IV—(Texts) Ed. by H. Krishna Sastri No. 227.

Puyal Vāykka Vaḷam Peruga; No reference to the Pandyan war. Sale of land (annı-
Year 5, day (3) 50
yanāmakarṇat-tittu) to Ammangai Alvar *alias Periyanacciyār, daughter of Kulōttunga-sōla-*deva who abolished the tolls (121 of 1888—S I. I IV—226).

Records gift of land at the hamlet of Manalur for two lamps to the temple of Tirukki-
Year 6
lanjedi-Mahadeva at Perumbaṛṛappuliyūr a taṇiyūr in Rajadhirajavalanadu (260 of 1913).

Begins with the introduction Puyal-vāyttu etc. Registers that a remission of taxes was
Year 7 and 20th day
made on the lands endowed after purchase by Udaiyañjevdāṉ Poṉṉambalakkūttan *alias* Vijayarājan, the headman of Vēlūr in Vendāḷai-Vēḷūr-Kuṟṟam, a sub-division of Rājēndrasoli-vaḷanādu, and Madhurāntakadevan Poṉṉamudaṉ of Śiṟukudi in Pāmbūrnādu, a sub-division of Uyyakkoṇdāı-vaḷanā lu for a flower garden for the god Āluḍiyār to be looked after by four gardeners and also for the maintenance of a guhai (monastery) for tapasvins (3 of 1936)

Registers an order of Toṇdaiman that an arrangement regarding a certain land
Year 7 and 225th day
made in order to provide flowers, coco nuts etc, be engraved on the wall of Vikramasōlan-tirumāligai (287of 1913)

(Tamil)—Begins with the same introduction. Registers the remission of taxes, granted
Year 7 and 240th day
by the King, on 3 vēlis and odd of lands endowed after purchase from the Mūlaparushai of Perumbaṟṟapuliyūr, an independent village in

Rājadhirāja-vaḷanādu, by Uyyavandān Tirumalapādi-udaiyān *alias* Toṇḍaiman of Kaḷattur in Eyilnādu for the maintenance of a flower-garden with five gardeners for the god. Rājēndrasinga-Mūvēdavēḷan figures as the Royal Secretary (4 of 1936).

Year 9 and 53th day Records a grant of land to the temple by a certain Kēralarajan for a flower garden. The inscription gives minute fractions of vēlis of land and land measures and it is therefore of value for the study of economic conditions of the time. (*vide* S I.I. Vol III 86). (457 of 1902).

Year 11 Records the King's sanction of a grant of land to the temple by a certain Valuvarāyan for the maintenance of a flower-garden. Regulation of the rights and duties of the tenants of the flower garden of the temple by the Mūlaparusai of Perumbaṟṟappuliyūr. Mentions Kaṇaku and Varik-kūṟuśeyvār. (458 of 1902).

Year 11 and 56th day Registers that certain lands granted by Gangayarayan were made tax-free and exempted from duties. The car procession was to be maintained and the temple was to receive 100 kasu as kudimai assessment and 6 kalam of paddy as vīrabhōga on each veli of land (294 of 1913.)

Year 11 and 115th day Registers the remission of taxes on the lands endowed after purchase from several individuals by Araiyaṉ Tāyilumnalla perumāl of Kaḷattūr in Eyil-nādu, a subdivision of Pāṇḍikulāśini-vaḷaṇādu, for rearing a garden called Tāvilumnallaperumal-tirunandavaṇam in Kadavāychcheri alias Tillaināyakanallūr, a hamlet of Perumbarrappuliyūr for the god These were included in the accounts under the devadhana lands (7 of 1936)

Registers that a certain Edirisolan alias
Year 12 and (Irungolan) having founded a temple called
125th day Vikramasolīśvaram-Udaiyar at Parakesarinallūr, a hamlet of Perumbarrappuliyūr after acquiring the required land from various people and having provided for houses of Brahmanas and temple servants, the king ordered the assessment on this land to be deducted from the revenue of the village to be entered in the temple accounts with the original documents preserved in the temple and the whole transaction engraved on the walls of the temple (309 of 1913)

Records gift of land for a flower-garden and its
Year 16 and servants, again the excess of land dis-
224th day covered by comparison with existing village accountants (varikkuriseyvār) were ordered to correct their figures, the servants of the garden were exempted from certain services usual to nibandakkarar. The tirumandira-ōlai was Rajanarāja(va)n-Muvendavelan (311 of 1913)

Records gift of interest on 1100 kāśu for maintaining a lamp and a lampstand. It was
Year 7 stipulated that the grant was to be renewed at the end of every 5 years, the principal being produced after each period before the mulaparusai (assembly) and the sthānattar (264 of 1913)

Seems to record the gift of a lamp—(265 of
Year 20 and 1913) Year 21 and 6th day Registers
121st day that a land was granted for a flower-garden

and another for maintaining its four servants; it was ordered that these lands might be included with the other temple lands and that the excess (madakku) in measurement be deducted from the village (accounts) The Tirumandira ōlai was Minavan-Muvendavelan (310 of 1913)

Year 3[illegible] and 160th day

Records that a gift of land for a flower garden called Ponnambalakkuthan in the village of Kōyilpundi, a hamlet of Perumbarrappulliyur was made to the temple of Aludaiyar by a certain Ponnambalakkuttan *alias* Nandipanman, he also provided for its upkeep by another gift of land made at Śerundimangalam which was a hamlet of Tyagavalli Chaturvedimangalam in Merka-nādu, these transactions and gifts were engraved on the walls of the temple by the order of the king's officers at the request of Nandipanman (273 of 1913)

Year 34 and 45th day

Registers that, at the request of the chiefs Pottappichchōlan and Kārānai Vilupperaiyan, the original documents pertaining to a gift of land which was made to the temple for a flower garden were preserved in the treasury of the temple and engraved on its walls (298 of 1913)

Year 34 and [illegible]nd day

'Who having been pleased to take Madurai, Karuvur, Ilam and the crowned head of the Pandya was pleased to perform the anointment of heroes' Registers gift of land for a flower garden It was ordered that the 4 servants of the garden must supply iruvāchchi, malligai, and nandiyavatta flowers to the temple regularly, when these failed other flowers had to be supplied (313 of 1913)

Records a number of lands which had been
Year 36 and 100th day granted for a flower-garden and were partly enjoyed by the servants of the garden were included at the donor's request in the tirunāmattukkani lands of the temple and the fact engraved on the temple walls.

The tirumandira-ōlai was Neriyudaichchola-Mūvēnda vēḷaṉ (who was one of the royal secretaries of Kulottunga III (301 of 1913).

Registers gift of land for a flower-garden to
Year 39 supply flowers to the temple of the goddess. Refers to a transaction which happened in the 33rd year of the King (314 of 1913).

Registers an order of three officers of the King,
Year 39 and 224th day *viz.* Toṇḍaiman, Tiruvaiyār-udaiyan, and Mathurantaka Brahma-Marayan that lands granted by a certain Laṅkēśvaran of Kiḷiyūr for providing 200 red lotuses to the temple and for maintaining the people that grew them was to be engraved on the walls of Vikramaśolan-tirumaligai. The Thirumandira-ōlai is stated to be Neriyudai-chchōla-Muvendavēḷaṉ; still another gift of land by the same person made for flower-garden in the 34th year and 52nd day of the king was also engraved, the old document having "become worn out." (284 of 1913).

An inscription in Tamil (north wall of the first
Undated prakara of the temple) undated registers an *order of Villavarayan* and four other officers assigning the income in paddy from certain land originally granted for the upkeep of a flower-garden, for the maintenance of the servants of the temple and of the flower-gardens (292 of 1913).

RĀJAKĒSARI RĀJARĀJA III

Year 2 and 14th day

Registers gift of land for providing flower-garlands to the temple. The grant was ordered to be engraved on the temple walls and the original documents deposited in the temple treasury. The royal secretary (Tirumandira-ōlai) was Rajendrasiṅga-Mūvēndavēḷaṉ. (299 of 1913).

Year 2 and 14th day

Registers gift of lands for a flower-garden and its servants by the donor mentioned in No. 299 (300 of 1913).

Year 3 and 57th day

Mentions the gift of land for a flower-garden by Umaiyaḷ, daughter of Vijayanuḷamban, chief of Nulambapādi *alias* Nigarilliśola-maṇḍalam. She had purchased the land from different people. The arrangement is ordered by some officials and three groups of temple authorities performing Śrikāryam, samudāyam and kōyilnāya-kam. Tirumandira-ōlai is Minavan-mūvēndavēlan (303 of 1913).

Year 3 and 115th day

Records gift of land at Vallam in Vēṇṇaiyūr-nādu, a sub-division of Rajādhirāja-vēḷa-nādu for supplying a garland of 130 lotuses every day. The document registering this grant was engraved under orders of Tondaimān, the Tirumandira-ōlai being Minavan Mūvēndavēḷaṉ (283 of 1913).

Year 3 and 204th day

Registers a similar endowment, for a flower-garden to the temple with four gardeners, of the lands which had been obtained by him as present from the mūlaparushaiyār of Perumbaṟṟappuliyūr, by Śomanāthadēva *alias* Uḍai-yārsvāmidēvar of Saṇḍilya-gōtra belonging to

Uttarāgrabāra in Uttarā-rāshtra in Uttarāpatha, after obtaining the royal sanction for the same (9 of 1936).

Year 3 and 224th day Registers gift of land for growing red lotuses and for providing food and cloth money to the gardeners who grew them. Refers to the land survey made in the 16th year of Śuṅgandavirtha Kulottuṅga-sōḷadeva and to the 25th year of Periyadēvar Tribhuvanavira-deva (317 of 1919).

Year 4 and 250th day Registers gift of land for the offering called 'tiruppāvāḍai on the day of Pushya in the month of 'Tai' to the god of Āḷudaiyār. The inscription was ordered to be engraved on the Kulōttuṅga-śōlan-tirumāligai by the Tirumandira-volai Rajanārāyana-Mūvēndavēlan (267 of 1913).

Year 9 and 85th day Register an order of the King's officers passed at the request of Gaṅgayarayan that certain lands granted to the temple for supplying flowers and maintaining the servants of the flower-gardens were to be made free of kuḍimai, that the documents pertaining to the lands in question were to be deposited in the temple treasury (tirukkaiotti ?) and that the transaction was to be engraved on the temple walls (306 of 1913).

Year 10 Registers the details of the land mentioned in a previous inscription which had been *purchased by the donatrix (14 of 1936).*

Year 10 and 121st day Records a gift, after purchase, of land in Erukkāttañjēri *alias* Jayaṅgondaśoḷanallūr, a hamlet of Perumbarrappuliyūr in Rājādhirājavaḷanāḍu by Tiruttalaiśēra-ninral, a maid servant of the royal household, for a flower-garden to the goddess. The order is signed by the Royal Secretary Minavan-Mūvēndavēlan (13 of 1936).

Records gift of land for supplying pomegranets and offerings to the God and Goddesses in the temple (548 of 1918).

Year 10 and 122nd day

Records gift of land by two private individuals for a flower-garden; provision was also made for the servants who looked after the garden (281 of 1913).

Year 10 and 235th day

Inscription in Tamil of Tribhuvanachakravartin Rajarajadeva registers that a flower garden had been founded for the benefit of the temple by a certain Karuppāruḍaiyāṇ *alias* Rājādhirājappallavaraiyaṇ at the hamlet of Koilpuṇḍi that land in three different villages had been granted for the maintenance of the gardeners who had to water the flower-plants, pick flowers and supply them to the temple, and that these lands were now included with other temple lands under orders of the king's officers, the transaction being engraved on temple walls and the original documents deposited in the temple treasury (316 of 1913).

Year 10 and 360th day

Records gift of land at Tirunirruchchōlamaṅgalam by a certain Kalingarayan, for supplying 500 jack fruits, 5,000 mangoes, and 5,000 plantains to the temple of Āḷuḍaiya-Nayanar. The assembly of that village agreed to make the land rent free by charging the taxes due on it, to the village. The Tirumandira-ōlai was Neṛivuḍaichchoḷa-Muvēndavelan (280 of 1913).

Year 14 and 107th day

Year 17 and 197th day

Records gift of garden land at Koyilpuṇḍi, a hamlet of Perumbaṟṟappuliyūr for providing garlands to the shrines of the god and the goddess by a certain Vāṇadhirajan. The order of the grant was as usual engraved on the walls of the temple (285 of 1913).

Year 17 and 272nd day

Records gift of land belonging to the village of Pāṇdur *alias* Kulōttuṅgaśōlan vallam in Rājadhirāja Vaḷanādu for maintaining the feeding house named Arapperuñjelviśolai at Perumbaṟṟappuliyūr in the west street called Muḍittalaikoṇḍa Perumāl-tiruvidhi (256 of 1913).

Year 24

(Damaged and beginning lost). Seems to register a similar endowment of land for the same purpose by another horse-dealer named Padappai Nārāyana-Nāyakan and engraved on the temple wall at the request of Vāṇādhirāja. Mentions the same royal secretary as a signatory (16 of 1936).

Year 24 and 350th day

(Slightly damaged). Registers an endowment of land after purchase, by a horse dealer (Kudirai chetti) named Senni-Nāyakan of Tālaipalli *for a flower garden for the temple*. The original sale deed and the present gift were engraved on the temple wall by royal order issued at the request of Vānādhirājan. Mentions the Royal Secretary Neṟiyuḍaichchōla-Mūvēndaveḷan (15 of 1936).

Year 24 and 364th day

Registers the royal order, issued at the request of Vāṇādhirājan, remitting certain taxes due on some land endowed as tirunandavanappuram *to the temple by* Maruṅgūr Vābhravyaṇ

Śokkapperumāṉ *alias* Rājarāja-Brahmamārayaı a resident of the Tirunilai-eḻugōpurapperuı deruvau at Perumbaṟṟappuliyūr for the daily suppl of flowers to the god Āḷudiya Nāyaṉār and hi consort. (1 of 1936).

Year 26 and 35th day Registers gift of 4¼ vēlis and odd of land calle Tillaināyaka-viḷāgam in Tiruchchiṟṟambalappatanam made by Muppuchchuṇḍāḷvı an aḍukkaḷaippendu (maid-servant of the royal household) for the maintenance of persons supplying flowers to the god and goddess and for conducting the *matha* built by her in the street leading to Edırilisōḷaṉ-tiruttōppu This gift was ratified at the request of the donatrıx by a royal order signed by the secretary Raje(ndrasola) Mūvēndavēḷaṉ. The land is said to have been originally granted (tax-free) ın the 7th year of the king to a certaın Gautaman Svāmikumāran. Arulāla Bhattan *alias* Savarnachakravartın of Uttamaśoḷamaṅgalam ın Rājādhırājaveḷanādu from whose sons the donatrix had purchased ıt. (8 of 1936)

Year 2 and 39th day Registers that an additional land was granted by a certain Kundaṉ *alias* Laṅkēśvara of Araśur for the maintenance of a flower-garden which had been already granted by himself for supplying 700 red lotuses to the temple every-day. The ten servants and a nāyaka who cultivated the garden were permitted to enjoy the land given them as a kāṇı. The transaction was engraved on the temple walls. (315 of 1913).

MISCELLANEOUS

An inscription ın Tamıl (on the door post of a new entrance cut close to the east gopura of the temple. The contents are the same as in No. 321 (324 of 1913).

An inscription in Tamil (on the gopura at the main entrance into the Sivakami Amman shrine in the temple. The contents are the same as in No. 321. (325 of 1913).

Maravarman Virakerala *alias* Kulasekhara deva; registers an order of Sediyarayan exempting certain lands granted for a flower-garden by a native of Palli Kodu in Malaimandalam, from paying Kadamai and Kudimai and declaring that these lands might enjoy the privileges of irrigation by channels, percolation and bailing. (350 of 1913).

Parakesarivarman *alias* Rajêndra Chola Dēva. (Not dated). Fragmentary. Begins with the introduction இரட்டபாடி ஏழரை இலக்கமும் etc., and stops with the name of the king. Three fragments found in the same place give the description and weight of jewels and utensils, besides mentioning the provision made for offerings to the god (610 of 1929—30).

Kulottunga Chola Deva. (48th year):—Fragmentary. Mentions Suttamalai-valanādu. Eight other fragments in the same place contain a portion of the historical introduction of two other Chola kings whose names are lost, and refers to gifts of money for offerings to the deity. (611 of 1929—30).

Rajamahendradeva (2nd year):—Fragmentary. Mentions Parantakan-Lokamahādēviyar Along with this are thirteen others, fragments of which record of gift of lands for offerings and special worship in the temple Three of these are in characters of the 16th century and one of them refers to a cell (for storing camphor) (612 of 1929-30)

Kōnērinmaikondan (3rd year and 5th day) — Incomplete Records royal orders to the Sabhā of Tiruvalundūr in Tiruvalundur-nadu about the lands belonging to the temple of Tirukkadavudaiyadeva *in that village (613 of 1929–30).*

Foundation by the Chola king of a temple for the glory of Solakulavalli and appears to make provision for singing the pāmālai (hymns) of the (Saiva saints) in the temple of Tirumulattanamudaiyan Also mentions the village of Kalumalam (341 of 1913).

In niches on the inner walls of the east gopura; these are labels engraved below images representing women in various dancing postures The inscriptions are in Sanskrit poetry (343 of 1913)

A record in Tamil on six fragments built into the platform forming steps in front of entrance to the temple One of the fragments bear the regnal year 48. The others refer to gift of lands (550 of 1918)

Registers gift of a village surnamed Pūrap pettai for meeting the expenses of one day during the Arpasi-pūram festivities in honour of the goddess (360 of 1913)

Damaged Built in at the beginning of the lines Refers to the procession of (the deity Pillaiyār Śolakēraladēva and his consorts and to gifts of land at Pañchavan madevilāgam in Mudigondaśolanallūr (614 of 1929–30)

One piece reads Śvasti Śri Vikramaśolan. About a dozen pillars in the mandapa bear the same label. One pillar bears the label 'Vikramaśolan-tirumandapam At the southern entrance to this mandapa are four pillars which bear the label Vira Paṇḍyan-tirumandapam.' (616 of 1930).

On some pillars in the hundred pillared mandapa in the temple

States that the mandapa (was the gift of) Akalankan. (109 of 1935).

Niches on the walls of the west gopura: In characters of the 13th century A. D, give the names of the images as follows:—Kāmadēvan Agastyan, Sridevi, Dēvēndran, Gaṅeśvarar and Durgādevi (21–26 of 1936)

Gives the names of the images as: Rudradêvar Rāhu-Kētukkaḷ, Nāradan, Aḷakēśvaran, Chandran Kṛiyāṣakti, Śanibhagavān and Vayubhagavān (27–34 of 1936).

Gives the names of the images as: Kshētrapāla-Piḷḷaiyār, Gaṁgādevi, Dhanvantari, (Tripura) sundari dēvī, Sukran, Vaijayan, Nāga, Yamunai, Bhadrakāi and Āḍichaṇḍēśvarar. (35–44 of 1936).

Gives the names of the images as: Niruti, Budhan, Jñānaśakti and Agnidēvan. Niches in the south wall of the west gopura of the Nataraja temple (45–48 of 1936) In characters of the 16th century A. D in the inner wall of the north gopura—gives the names of the four figures sculptured below these labels as follows:—(1) Viruddagiriyil Śēvakapperumal (2) His son Visuvamutt(u) (3) Tiruppiṟaikkodai Āchāri Tirumarungan and (4) his brother Kāraṇāchari (7–20 of 1936).

Right of the entrance in the east gopura of the temple—a Tamil verse (modern)—(173 of 1892).

MEDIAEVAL PANDYAS

JATAVARMAN SUNDARA PANDYA

Year 6 and 26th day Contains some detailed account of land measurement.

A record of Sundara Pandya in the form of a Sanskrit verse. (For text, Vide S. I. I. Vol. IV (Texts). Ed. by H. Krishna Sastri, No. 625).

Year 7 and 230th day

It opens with the usual Sanskrit *birudas* of Sundara-Pandya whose vassal the donor appears to have been. For text, Vide S. I. I. Vol. IV (Texts) Ed. by H. Krishna Sastri No. 624 (176 of 1892).

Year 7 and 236th day

The first ten lines are engraved over another inscription of Vikrama-Choladeva beginning with the historical introduction பூமாலை மிடைந்து etc.; order of Toṇḍaimān to the temple authorities remitting certain taxes on lands which had been originally granted for the maintenance of the servants of a flower-garden belonging to the temple; the reason for the remission was that the *said lands being close to the sea had become filled up with sand overgrown with weeds*; mentions Vira-rākshasa-Vēlaikkārar. (289 of 1913).

Year 7 and 252nd day

Contains order of Kalappaḷarayar to register as tirunamathukkāni, certain lands granted for conducting festivals and providing offerings in the temple of Tiruchirrambala-Māhāli which was founded on the south side of the

Year 8

road by which the God was taken in procession for the sea-bath and to engrave the same on stone (297 of 1913).

Records gift of land, order of Villavadaraiyan Year 9 and 200th day approving of certain arrangements about specified temple lands made by the assembly (mūlaparushaiyār) of Perumbaṟṟappuliyūr (288 of 1913).

Registers an order remitting assessments on Year 11 and 56th day certain lands granted to the temple for a flower-garden. The transactions were engraved on Vikramaśōlan-tirumaligai (293 of 1913).

Registers remission of taxes on some lands Year 12 and 175th day endowed after purchase in Erukkāttañjeri *alias* Jayaṅgonda Śoḷanallūr, a hamlet of Perumbaṟṟappuliyūr in Madurāntakappērilamai-nādu by Araiyaṉ Niṟaṉi-Pavalakuṉṟar *alias* Śoḷagaṅagan, the headmen of Maṉarpākkam in Toṇḍaimaṇḍalam, for rearing a flower-garden called 'Kuṉranāyakaṉ-Tirunandavanam' for the god and the goddess for the maintenance of the gardeners. The signatory is Gāṅgayarāya. (6 of 1931).

Registers the founding of an agrahāra named Year 13 Vikramapaṇḍya-Chaturvēdimaṅgalam on the western side of Perumbaṟṟappuliyūr and its presentation to 108 learned Brahmaṇas. For the maintenance of these and of other village accessories (grāmaparikara) the village Rajaśikhamaninallūr *alias* Puliyaṅkudi on the western bank of Poṉṉeri was acquired and granted, being divided into 147¾ shares (*pangu*). (277 of 1913).

It is incomplete and registers another order of
Year 14 and 124th day Villavarayan with reference to certain grants of land providing flower-gardens to the god and goddess; one of these latter was situated in Vikramaśolanallūr (also called Akkaṉpaḷḷippaḍai) near Perumbaṟṟappuliyūr and was granted by Śvamidēvar, still another grant of land, in the hamlet of Kōlam *alias* Śolakēraladēvanallūr was made for providing offerings on the occasion when the images were taken on procession to the sea. (275 of 1913)

Records an order of Villavarāyan and other
Year 15 and 363rd day officers of the king that the maintenance of worship and offerings in the temple of Dēvargal-Nayaṉar was to be met from certain grants of land made to that temple. *(274 of 1913)*

Registers an order of Kulaśēkhara-Śolakaṉ
Year 17 and 60th day remitting the taxes on three vēli of land got in exchange and granted for a flower-garden by Pāṇḍyan *alias* Narasiṅgadēva of Mayindapuram in Pāṇḍi-maṇḍalam. (10 of 1936).

A record of Sundara-Pandya in Sanskrit verse.
Not dated (For text, *vide* S. I. I. Vol. IV texts Ed. by H. Krishna Sastri, No. 632)-(184 of 1892).

A record of Sundara-Pandya in Sanskrit and Tamil. The inscription is incomplete. For text, *vide* S. I. I. Vol. IV (texts) Ed. by H. Krishna Sastri, No. *631*—*(183 of 1892)*.

Records of Sundara-Pandya in Sanskrit verse (For texts, *vide* S. I. I. Vol. IV (texts) Ed. by H. Krishna Sastri Nos. 626, 627, 628, 629, 630)—
—(178 to 182 of 1892).

Two verses the first of which refers to a conquest of the Pandya king over the Chola, the latter being driven into the forest. The second mentions Kadavarkon and the Pandya King Sundarathōl, (332 of 1913).

Tamil verse—one verse in praise of Sundara-Pandya and his weighing himself against gold (338 of 1913).

Tamil verse—glorifies the prowess of Sundara-Maṛaṇ (*i.e.* Sundara Pândya) who annihilated the fôrces of the Telingas that surrounded him and drove the Bana chief into the forest (340 of 1913).

Three verses describing the glory of King Sundara-Pāṇḍya who conquered the kings of Veṇādu (*i.e.* Travancore), those of the North (*i.e.* the Telingas) and those of the Kongu (country) and killed Gandagopila. (354 of 1913).

Tamil verse contains 3 verses and refers to the fight between Sundara Pandya and the Telingas at Mudugur in which the dead bodies were strewn up to the bank of the Peraru. (361 of 1913).

Tamil verse consists of two verses. There is apparently a reference to Sundara-Pandya's weighing himself against gold and using it for covering the temple. (363 of 1913).

A record of Sundara-Pandya I—Tamil verse (171 and 172 of 1892).

Relates to Pandya dynasty and the name of the king is Jatavarman. Registers a gift of land as Jivite to a number of persons who had to work after the garden called Sundara Pāṇḍyan-tirutōppu and the street called Sundarapāṇḍyan-teṅgutiruvidhi. Mentions the king's officers Teṉṉavan-Brahmarayan, Vikramaśōla Brahmarāyar, Vikrama-Pāṇḍya-Brahmarayar, Jayatuṅga-pallavarāyar, Villavarayar, Kurukulatharayar. (546 of 1918).

MARAVARMAN KULASEKHARA DEVA

Records an order of Chēdiyarāyan to engrave
Year 5 and 353rd day on the temple walls a gift of land for providing offerings etc., in a shrine situated in one of the streets of Perumbaṟṟappuliyūr. (286 of 1913).

Year 23 Ko-Maravarman Tribhuvanachakravartin Kulasekhara-deva. (124 of 1888).

Maravarman Tribhuvanachakravartin Kula-
Year 28 and 190th day sekharadeva. There are stones missing in the middle. Registers an order of Kaliṅgarāyan granting lands for the maintenance of certain flower-gardens one of which was called Ayyanangakāṟan tirunandavanam (547 of 1918).

Maravarman Kulaśekhara; registers an order
Year 19 of Kaliṅgarāyan. Provides for offerings to the god Kulottung-śoḷa-Vinayaka-Piḷḷaiyar who is enshrined on the south side of the seven storeyed gopura of Rajakkal-tambiran-tirumaligai; refers to Ellāndalaiyan-Perumāḷ-śandi. (366 of 1913).

Maṟavarman Vikrama-Pandyadeva: contains
Year 4 and 18th day order of Kulaśēkhara-śoḷakaṉ exempting duties and assessments of lands presented by certain Chediyarayan for maintaining 36 persons employed in a water-shed in the 'maṇḍapa

known as Ānaiyeṟṟukkūdam south of the seven storeyed gopura on the east side of Rājakkal-tambiran tirumāligai, 54 persons who prepared offerings for the god, 32 learned Brahmanas, 54 persons who prepared offerings at Sīkāli (*i. e.* the shrine of the goddess?) and lastly the temple supervisors. (295 of 1913).

Year 5 and 270th day — Registers that, under orders of Gangēyarayan land was granted for supplying garlands on the occasion of the service called Rājākkalnāyan-Śandi after the king, and on the day of the festival called Rājākkalnāyanperiya-tirunāḷ. (270 of 1913)

Year 6 and 355th day — Registers an order of Veṅgattaraiyan to the temple authorities to engrave on the walls of Vikrama-śolan-tirumāligai the gift of lands in Paḷḷippadai *alias* Vikramaśōḷanāllur, Erukkāṭṭañjeri *alias* Jayaṅgondaśolanaḷḷūr and Manalūr *alias* Jayaṅkondaśolanaḷḷūr for the flower-garden of Ulagamuḷudumuḍaiyal-tirunandavanam which was so named after the queen. (276 of 1913).

Year 7 — Registers an order of Vangattaraiyan. Gift of land for supplying plantain fruits. (549 of 1918).

VIKRAMA-PANDYA

Not dated — A record in the east gopura (123 of 1888).

Not dated — Three verses extolling Vikrama-Pāṇḍya. The first says that he conquered the king of Veṇaḍu (*i. e.* Travancore) at Podiyil. In the second he is addressed as Bhuvanēkavira and Koṟkai-Kavala and is stated to have been the enemy of Ganapati. The third advises the king Vikrama-Pāṇḍya not to go to the north; for there 'it says' is a foe—a woman ruling with a man's name. (365 of 1913).

Not dated Tamil verse in praise of the Pandya King (Mīnavan) Vikrama-Pāṇḍya (353 of 1913).

Not dated Tamil verse contains three verses the first of which refers to a battle fought on the banks of Vellaru in which a certain Bhuvanekaviran was victorious. The last refers to Vikrama Pandya. (336 of 1913).

Inscription in Tamil verse—one verse describing the anger of Vikrama Pandya. (337 of 1913).

MARAVARMAN VIRA PANDYA

Year 4 and 123rd day Registers an order of Śēdiyarayaṉ that the gift of garden lands made by a certain Villavadaraiyan together with lands provide for the maintenance of 18 servants of the garden and of the water-shed within it may be engraved on the temple-walls (351 of 1913).

Year 4 and 192nd day Registers an order of Pallavarāyan to the temple authorities to engrave on the walls of Kulottunga-śōlan-tirumaligai a gift of land for offerings to the shrine Alagiya-Tiruchchiṟṟambalamudaiyar built by a Brahman at the hamlet of Koṟṟangudi *alias* Pavitramaṇikyanallūr. (279 of 1913)

Year 8 and 57th day Maravarman Tribhuvanachakravartin Vīra-Pandya deva. Registers that under the orders of Vikrama-Pāṇḍya Gāṅgēyarāyan some land was set apart for building a quarter to be inhabited exclusively by the weavers (Śoliya-śāliyar) and named Teriyavaranınraperumal-puram on condition that these weavers supplied few new cloths (every year) to the goddess Siva-kamasundari on the day of the tiruppudiyidu festival and five other small cloths for the shrine of Tirugnānasambandar (269 of 1913)

Year 9 and 166th day Registers an order of Vīra Pāndya Vanadhi-rayan that gift of one tiruvōdai together with a piece of land for the maintenance of the latter made by a certain Dipattaraiyan at Śolakulavallinallur and added to the devadāna lands of the temple and that the transaction may be engraved on the temple wall (320 of 1913).

Year 12 Registers a grant of land after purchase in Erukkāttañjēri, a hamlet of Perumbarrap-puliyur, made by Atkkondān *alias* Narā vanadevan of Ilāngudi *alias* Indravatāranallur in Tenvalliitturukkai situated in Pāṇdi mandalam, for a flower garden to the temple of Tiruchchirram-balam-Udaiyār (5 of 1936)

PAṆDYA KING MARAVARMAN VĪRA PĀṆDYA

Date is lost Consists of a number of mutilated and uncon-nected pieces, refers to an arrangement (vyavastha) made by the temple managers. (328 of 1913).

Inscription of Tamil verse, in praise of the Pandya king Mentions Kudal (*i e.* Madura)—(357 of 1913)

Consists of six verses of which five refer to a battle fought evidently at Chidambaram by a certain Munaiyaṉ Vallıvān Adittaṉ, chief of Panaiśeyyar on behalf of the Pāṇḍya (Minavaṉ) against the' Chola (Vaḷavan). The author of the poem was ' Taynalla-Perumal-Munaiyadaraiyan *alıas* Bhuvanēka Vıra Tondaiman.

Pandyan Inscrıption—A Tamil verse (170 of 1892).

KOPPERUNJINGA

An inscription (south wall of the 'mandapa' in front of the Tıllaıyamman shrıne) ın Tamil of Kopperunjıngadeva. Records sale of land for 2,100 naṟkāśu (397 of 1903).

Year 2 and 13th day

An ınscription (north wall of the 'mandapa' in front of the Tıllaiyamman shrine) in Tamıl. Records sale of land for 28,000 kāśu. Refers to the temple treasury called 'Tıllaıvanamuḍaiya Paramēśvarı Bandhāram'. (399 of 1903)

Year 3

An ınscriptıon (south wall of the 'mandapa' ın front of the Tıllaiamman shrine) in Tamıl. Records sale of land. The king's name is not mentıoned. (395 of 1903).

Year 3

An ınscriptıon (on the north wall of the central shrıne in the Tıllaiyamman shrıne) records sale of land for 28,000 kāśu (anṟaḍu Śellam Naṟkāśu)—Mentıons 'Vılaıpıramānattıttu'. (393 of 1903)

Year 3

An inscrıption (on the south wall of the central, shrine ın the Tıllaıyamman temple) in Tamıl recordıng sale of land *The Kıng's name ıs not mentioned.* (392 of 1903)

Year 3

An inscription (east wall of the central shrine in the Tillaiyamman temple) in Tamil of Sakalabhuvana chakravartin Kopperunjingadeva Records gift of land bought for 37,000 kāśu to Nācciyār 'Tillaivanamudaiya Paramēśvari' as Tirunāttukkani. (390 of 1903).

Year 3

An inscription in Tamil (north wall of the second 'prakara' of the temple) of Sakalabhuvanachakravartin Kopperunjingadeva. Records gift of land—Gift for a flower garden. (Compare Epi. Indi. Vol. VII, p. 166)—(462 of 1902).

Year 3 and 325th day

An inscription in Tamil (on the east wall of the central shrine in the Tillaiyamman temple) of Sakalabhuvana Chakravartin Kopperunjingadeva. Records sale of land. Mentions "Villaipiramānt-Tiṭṭu". (391 of 1903).

Year 3 and 25th day

An inscription in Tamil (north wall of the second prakara of the temple) of Kopperunjingadeva. Records an order of Śoḷakān—Provision for feeding and clothing 50 persons (toppukkuḍigal) employed for the maintenance of a flower-garden. Gift for a cow-stall (tirukkōśālai) —Also mentions measure Śelvi Rāja Kēsaari. (465 and 466 of 1902).

Year 3 and 81st day

An inscription (north base of the 'mandapa' in front of the Tillaiyamman shrine) in Tamil of Kopperunjingadeva records sale of land. (394 of 1903).

Year 5

An inscription (north wall of the 'mandapa' in front of the Tillaiyamman shrine) in Tamil of Kopperunjingadeva. Records

Year 5

sale of land for 50,000 "anrāḍu-śel-kāśu" (398 of 1903)

An inscription in Tamil (west wall of the first
Year 5 'prakara') of Sakalabhuvanachakravartin Kopperunjingadeva, dated 5th year Records an order of Sōlakōn of Aragūr *alias* Perumal Pillai, one of the King's chief officers Gift of lands. (459 of 1902).

Two inscriptions in Tamil (north wall of the
Year 5 second 'prakara' of the temple) of Sakalabhuvanachakravartin Kopperunjingadeva Records an order of Sōlokōn Refers (463 of 1902) to the construction of south gopura 464 of 1902 refers to gift of lands bought for 3,000 kāśu for digging a pond—(Perumal Tiruvodai) for growing flowers The Attur record on the same subject [Attur record 285 of 1921 of Kopperunjinga—Gift of the village of Attur by Alagiya Śīyan Avani—Alappīṛandan Kādavan Kopperunjinga for building the southern entrance of the temple of Tiruccirrambalam udaiyar at Perumbarrappuliyur (Chidambaram) as a gōpura of seven storeys, named Sokkaccīyan]

Tamil (damaged)—Registers a grant of lands
Year 5 and 33rd day in different places made after purchase by Rāvalar Śrīkayilāsadēvar of the [Golа] Kimaṭha at Tiruvannāmalai for the maintenance of a flower garden with four gardeners for the temple The King's order of approval is signed by Śolakọṇ (West wall of the third prakara of the Nataraja temple, right of entrance A. R E 11 of 1936)

Registers an order signed by Śolakōn sanction-
Year 5 and 234th day ing a similar endowment of land after
purchase, made for rearing a flower garden
for the temple by Ponnambalakuthan Tulaiyāda-śelvan *alias* Kurukkaliāyan of Palaiyur *alias* Rajēndraśōlanallūr in Pālaiyūr-nadu, a subdivision of Uṟṟukkāṭṭu-Koṭṭam, a district in Jayangonda-solamandalam (West wall of the third prakara of the Nataraja temple, right of entrance. (A. R E 12 of 1936)

An inscription in Tamil (north wall of the
Year 6 second prakara of the temple) of Koppe-
runjingadeva. Registers an order of
Śolakōn that certain arrangements made by the temple authorities and the village assembly recording the gift of a flower garden and the maintenance of its servants may be engraved on the temple (296 of 1913)

An inscription in Tamil (north wall of the
Year 7 second prakara of the temple) of Koppe-
runjingadeva dated 7th year Registers
an order of Śōlakōn recording gift of land for a flower-garden by a dancing girl (304 of 1913)

An inscription in Tamil (north wall of the
Year 7 second prakara) of Kopperunjingadeva
Registers an order of Śōlokōn that eight
śandi oblations like those offered at the shrine of mūlasthanam-Udaiyar in (the temple) of Tiru-Chirrambalam be also offered at the shrine of Dakshinamūrti and that the gift of land made for providing five of these eight śandis be made tax-free (305 of 1913)

An inscription in Tamil (north wall of the
Year 8 second prakara of the temple) of Kopperunjingadeva registers an order of Śōḷakōṇ that the Śaliya merchants (nagara) were to be provided with land for building their houses on condition that they would supply the necessary clothes for the pariśaṭṭam of the God and Goddess. (308 of 1913).

An inscription (north wall of the Tillaiyamman
Year 8 shrine) in Tamil of Kopperunjingadeva mentions the temple of Vāranavāśi-Mādēvar and records sale of land to Chōḷakkōṇar for building a temple of Piḍāriyār (401 of 1903)

An inscription in Tamil (west wall of the
Year 8 second prakara of the temple) of Sakala-bhuvanachakravartin Kopperunjingadeva. Records an order of Śōḷakōṇ—Gift of lands for constructing ponds for providing flowers (Sēngaluṇīr) to the God and Goddess. (460 of 1902).

Inscription in Tamil (north wall of the second
Year 9 prakara) of Kopperunjingadeva. Registers an order of Perumal Pillai *alias* Śōḷakoṇ that certain gifts of land for the maintenance of gardeners be recorded on the temple walls (318 of 1913).

An inscription in Tamil (north wall of the
Year 10 and 9th day second prakara of the temple) of Kopperunjingadeva Registers an order of Perumal Pillai *alias* Śōḷakōn made for the welfare of the king; records an exchange of land and refers incidentally to the temple (Śri Koil) of the Piḍāri called Tiruchchiṟṟambala-Māhāḷi on the south side

of the street called Vikkiramaśolan-terguttiruvīdi by which the god was taken on procession to the sea (312 of 1913)

An inscription in Tamil (same as 326 of 1913)
Year 10 Order of Śōlakōn—Gift for a flower-garden, and for sacred offerings to Aṇdābharana devar. (327 of 1913).

Registers an order of Śōlakon relating to the
Year 1 [1] gift of land in Erukkāttuchcheri *alias* Jayangoṇdaśōlanallūr in Kidāiangoṇdośola—Pērilamainādu to the east of Perumbarrappuliyūr by purchase, by Iravalar Kayilāyodevan of the northern matha at Tiruvaṇṇāmalai, for the expenses of providing tiruppāvādai during Tai-pūśam festival and for flower-garden for the supply of flowers to the God (West wall of the second prakara in the Nataraja temple) (A R E 106 of 1936)

Tamil (damaged) Records an order of Śōlakōn
Year 1 [1] exempting from taxes, certain lands endowed to the temple for providing the tiruppāvādai offerings to Tirukkāmakkōttamudaiya-Periyanāchchiyar, by two women (names lost). (West wall of the second prakara in the Nataraja temple) (A R E. 107 of 1935)

Registers an order of Śōlakōn making a gift of
Year 1 [1] several lands for the merit of the king, for supplying flowers to the God and for the maintenance of the gardeners rearing them (West wall of the second prakara in the Nataraja temple) (A R E 108 of 1935)

Among the several important officers of Kopperunjingadeva, two officers figure largely in

Chidambaram inscriptions–Araśūraḍaiyāṉ Śeṅgaṇivāyan *alias* Sōḷakōṉ who is stated to be an officer (mudali) of Peruñjinkadēva (No. 108) and his brother Vēṇāḍadaiyān (No 104).

An inscription in Tamil (in the Bhimeśvara temple Siṅgaratoppu, near Chidambaram)
Year 11 of Kopperunjinga records sale of 9 ma of land, for 5,000 kasu to the temple of Nayanar Tirukkālanjedi-Udaiyar at Paṇṇaṅguḍichcheri *alias* Parakesarinallur, a hamlet of Perumbaṟṟappuliyūr. The land sold was a field of the western hamlet of Iḷaṅangur and the sale was witnessed by the assembly of the village. (261 of 1913).

An inscription in Tamil (east wall of the Mahishāsuramardani shrine in the temple)
Year 12 of Kopperunjingadeva registers an order of Śōḷakōn that a gift of land made for a flower garden to the shrine of Aṇḍabaraṇadeva be engraved on the wall of the shrine and the original documents connected therewith be kept in the temple treasury. (326 of 1913).

An inscription (north wall of the second prakara of the temple) of Kopperunjinga-
Year 12 deva registers an order of Perumāḷ Pillai *alias* Śōḷakōn and mentions the gift of land for a flower-garden. (302 of 1913).

An inscription (south wall of the mandapa in front of the Tillaiyamman shrine) in Tamil.
Year 14 The King's name is not mentioned. It provides for the supply of saffron etc., required for the temple of Tillaivaṉamuḍaiya-Paramēsvari. (396 of 1903).

An inscription (south and east walls of the
Year 16 Bhairava shrine in the Tillaiyamman temple) in Tamil, of Kopperunjingadeva records an order of Śōḷakōn (400 of 1903).

Inscription in Tamil (north wall of the second
Year 16 prakara of the temple) of Kopperunjingadeva. Records (467 of 1902) an order of Śōḷakōn. Gift for a flower-garden called Śokkacciyan Kamuku tirunandavanam, (468 of 1902) also records a gift for a flower-garden called Śeṅganivāyan tirunandavanam. (467 and 468 of 1902).

An inscription in Tamil (north wall of the
Year 17 second prakara of the temple) of Kopperunjingadeva Registers an order of Śōḷakōn that a gift of land was made for additional offerings in the shrine of Dakshinamūrti dēva (referred to in No. 305) and that this land was made a rent-free tirunāmattukkāni unddr the command of the king. (307 of 1913)

(Tamil) registers an order of Śōḷakōn that as the
Year 19 garden called Sokkaśiyan-Kamugu-tirunandavanam which had been endowed in the 15th year of Periyadēvar was found to measure 16 ma and odd in excess as measured by the Sokkachchiyaṉ-kōl, this additional land be also entered as belonging to the garden, the additional taxes assessed on this land being remitted. (On the north wall of the second prakara in the Nataraja temple—A. R. E. 103 of 1935).

Registers an order of Śōḷakōn exempting from
[1] 9th year certain taxes the lands given by Gaṅgōḷi, Tiruchchiṟṟambalam-Udaiyār *alias* Udaiyār Iśvarśivar of Dakshiṅaradha in Uttarāpatha, for

the maintenance of the gardeners employed in the flower-garden called Tiruchchirrambalamudaiyān-tirunandavanam which was formed by him for the use of the temple. (West wall of the second prakara in the Nataraja temple—A.R E. 105 of 1935).

Inscription in Tamil (north wall of the second *19th year* prakara) of Kopperunjingadeva registers that Śōlokōn ordered that a gift of land for a grove of trees be made a rent-free dēvadāna and to be registered on the temple walls (319 of 1913).

An inscription in Tamil (west wall of the first *Year 34* prakara of the temple) of Sakalabhuvana-chakravartin. Records an order of Vēṇaḍudaiyan, brother of Śōlokōn. Gift of land as dēvadāna—free of rent for temple service to Goddess-Avani Āḷaapiranda Nācciyar. (461 of 1902)

An inscription (west wall of the second prakara *Year 36* of the temple) in Tamil characters of Sakalabhuvanachakravartin Kōpperunjingadeva. Records gift of land—Arrangements for car festival service etc., made by Assembly of Chidambaram out of lands presented by land-accountant (nilak-kannaku) Danmappiriyan and Tillai Mūvāyira Vēlān See S. A. 124 and 329 for details. (455 of 1902)

(Tamil) Registers an order of Vēṇādudaiyān, *Year 36* exempting from taxes the 10 veli of land which had been granted after purchase by Tiruvaiyārudaiyār for services on several festive occasions to the god (Nāyakar)—West wall of the second prakara in the Nataraja temple (A. R. E 104 of 1935.

An inscription in Tamil (west wall of the first
Year 36 prakara of the temple) of Sakalabhuvana-chakravartin Kopperunjingadeva records an order of Vēnāḍuḍaiyan referring to gift of land (456 of 1902)

An inscription in Tamil (on a pillar of the
Undated Western entrance into second prakara, left side) states that this pillar of the entrance was presented by Perumaḷ *alias* Śōḷakōnar, one of the chiefs of Kopperunjingadeva for (the merit of) his master. (321 of 1913)

VIJAYANAGARA KINGS

Inscription in Tamil and Grantha (west
Undated gopura of Virabhūpatiraya, registers that 64 cows were granted for maintaining perpetual lamps in the presence of Nṛittanātha by the ministers Chauṇḍarasa and Ādittarasa. (358 of 1913)

(On the north wall of the Karpagavinayakar
Saka 1349 temple at the western gopura of the temple) of the Vijayanagara king Virapratapa Dēvaraya—Mahārāya, registers that the king ordered certain irregularities in temples and temple lands to be set right (376 of 1913)

(On a second pillar of the western entrance
Saka 1422 into second prakara of the temple records that Tirumalaikkolundar the agent of Narasā-Nayaka while he was in charge of the temple enforced that ten cake offerings and betel leaves which must be distributed among certain

specified individuals for the merit of Narasa-Nayaka were not to be withheld from them and used otherwise. (322 of 1913).

(South gopura of the temple) of Vīrapratapa
Saka 1425 Tammaraya (Saluva dynasty) records that a certain Moṇḍukoli Rāmanayākar Mallanayakkar gave the village of Karikkudi, the western hamlet of Perumbaṟṟappuliyūr for a double garland and offerings to be offered every day (344 of 1913). (345 of 1913). Tamil verse. Much damaged. Mentions Por-Puliyur.

(Southern entrance into the first prakara left
Saka 1432 side) of the Vijayanagara king, Vīrapratapa Vira-Krishṇayadeva Mahārāya dated Saka 1432 records gift of three villages with an income of 1400 rēkai (gadyāna) for the mahapuja in the temple of Aḷagiya Tiruchchiṟṟambalam-uḍaiya-Tambiraṇar (included in Araśu-kiḷpaṟṟu a sub-division of Veṇṇaiyur-naḍu in Rajadhiraja Velanaḍu which was itself a district on the northern bank (of the Coleroon) included in the province of Bhuvanēka Viran-pattanaśirmai and for the maintenance of a feeding house by a certain Appa Piḷḷai. (323 of 1913)

(East gopura of the temple) of Krishnaraya;
Saka 1444 records that a certain Mangaraśan granted the village of Chidambaranāthapuram (to the temple)—(333 of 1913)

Krishnadeva—Records the building of the
Undated gopura (left of the entrance to the north gopura of the temple) (174 of 1892).

Krishnadevaraya (left of the entrance to the
Undated north gopura of the temple)—Sanskrit version of No. 174. (175 of 1892).

(On a slab built into the floor in front of the
Undated Ganapati shrine in the temple); refers to a gift by purchase of some godowns by a certain Nāgama-Nayaka. (331 of 1913).

Achyutadevaraya—(Sanskrit in Grantha and
Saka 1451 Virodhi, Phalguna Tamil) Records that on a representation made by Sāluva Daṇṇāyaka, the income from 82 specified villages amounting to 3,000 poṉ which had been originally allotted by Krishnaraya Nayaka for the expenses of the car and other festivals and for repairs to the temple of Chidambarēśa at Perumbaṟṟappuliyūr was re-endowed by the King and was left in charge of a *tapasvin* named Periyadēvar. (This Krishnaraya Nayaka was evidently an officer of the king.) (West wall of the second prakara of the Nataraja temple) (A. R. E 2 of 1936)

(North tier of the central shrine in the Govin-
Saka 1460 daraja Perumal temple) of Achyutadeva Mahārayā. Unfinished; records the reconsecration of Govindarajasvamin at Chitrakuta by Achytarāya. (1 of 1915)

(South wall of the first prakara of the Nataraja
Saka 1461 temple) of the Vijayanagara king *Achutayya Mahārayā.* The king ordered that the image of Tillai-Govindarāja Perumal at Perumbaṟṟappuliyūr in Valudalam bathu-uśāvadi, a subdivision of Vennaiyūr-nādu in Rājādhiraja valanādu might be set up according to the ritual of Vaikānasa-stura and granted 500 poṉ which was 'the

income from four villages for the upkeep of daily worship (272 of 1913).

Saka 1489 (On a slab lying near the Paśupatiśvara temple at Tiruvetkalam, Chidambaram) Akshaya, Tai 25th day; records gift of the village of Tiruvētkalam to the shrines Chidambarēśvara and Śivakamisundari Amman of the Tirumūlasthānam temple by Achchutappa-Nayaka, son of Śiru-Sevvappa-Nayaka for the merit of Tirumalairājayan i. e., the Karnata king Tirumala I)—(259 of 1913).

Saka 1500 Virapratāpā Venkatadeva Mahārayā; Records gift of 4 villages to the temple of Chidambarēśvara and Śivakamasundari Ammal to provide oblations and sacred bath in early mornings for the merit of Vaiyappa-Krishṇappa-Koṇḍama-Nāyakar. (334 of 1913).

Saka 1503 (South gopura) of Śrirangadeva-Maharaya II. Registers gift of seven villages and of income from pepper trade called *miḷagu-taragu* for oblations and festivals in the shrine of the god and goddess by Vaiyappa-Krishṇappa Koṇḍama-Nāyaka (48 and 349 of 1913).

Saka 1510 (South gopura) of Venkatadeva-Mahāraya (346 of 1913).

Saka 1510 (South gopura) of Venkatadeva Maharaya records that the provision made by Vaiyappa-Krishṇappa-Koṇḍama-Nāyaka for 20 offerings to be distributed among the Śaiva mendicants (*paradēśi*) in the temple, was placed under the supervision of Namaśivāya Uḍaiyār, the "superintendent of all services (Kaṭṭalai)" (349 and 362 of 1913).

(North gopura) of Venkatadeva-Mahārayā; registers that Vīrapratāpa Krishnadeva-Mahāraya after having started on a campaign against Simadri-Pottunuru planted a pillar of victory there and returning thence he paid a visit to Ponnambalam (i e, Chidambaram) worshipped the god and built the northern *gopura* of the temple. (371 of 1913)

Saka 1510

(East gopura) of the temple right of entrance of Venkatadēva Mahārayā; registers that Vaiyappa-Krishnappa - Kondama - Nāyaka ordered that the 30 (rice) offerings for which he had provided 50,000 *kalams* of paddy in the district of Viranarāyanachchirmai, to be distributed among Śaiva mendicants (*tiruottunayanmar*)—(339 of 1913)

Saka 1510

Of Venkatadēva Mahārayā, records gifts of 300 pon for providing 20 (rice) offerings to the god Chidambarēśvara and distributing the same among begging devotees It is stated that this amount was till then being set apart by the temple for the *ulakkai* and *Korru* of the king and his followers (Rajagaram ?)—(335 of 1913)

Saka 1510

(On a slab near the west gopura) of Venkatadeva-Maharāya, registers that for the merit of Vaiyappa-Krishnappa-Kondama-Nāyaka the districts of Devamandalasirmai, Vīranārayanachcīrmai, Terku-nādu Vadakku-nādu, the five villages grouped under Aśuvūr and all others that had been enjoyed by the temple of Chidambarēśvara from early times were made tax-free and that a fresh provision was made for a daily offering of 750 *taligai* (369 of 1913)

Saka 1515

(On a slab up near the south gopura); provided for some specified repairs to the temple made for the merit of Muttukṛishnappa-Nāyaka, son of Vaiyappa-Kṛishṇappa-Kondama Nāyaka. Also mentions a *mandapa* on the bank of Kollidavāru built by the same donor. (352 of 1913).

Saka 1520

Tamil verse (north gopura). Records that the three gopuras were the gifts of kings who wore a crown. This the northern gopura was built by the god himself. The poet evidently means to say that this is the best of the four. (374 of 1913). We know from No. 371 that Krishnaraya built it.

(East wall of the first prakara of the Naṭarāja temple); of the Vijayanagara King Mahā-maṇḍalesvara Sri Raṅga Rāya III); records that the king repaired the big mandapa, in front of the Tillai Gōvindarājaśvāmin shrine in Tiruchitrakūdam, the gopura of the shrine, the vimānas of the goddesses Puṇḍarikavalli nāchchiyār and Śuḍikkodutta nāchchiyār and the 'mandapa' in front of Tiruvāli-Alvan. He is also stated to have made rent-free the five villages of Ādūr, Karuṅguḷi, Kuriyāmaṅgalam, Marudāntanallūr and Uḍaiyūr in which the Śri-Vaishṇavas were permanently living. (271 of 1913).

Saka 1565

MISCELLANEOUS

(West gopura) of Cochin Ramavarma-Maharaya of the family of Śēraman-Perumal-Nayanār (Saka 1498) The King is stated to have been born under the asterism Viśāka. Provides for 33 *taligai* (offerings) to be offered to Ānandatāṇḍava Perumal Nayaṇār and distributed among Brahmaṇas, Mahēśvaras and the temple cooks. (350 of 1913)

SOUTH GOPURA

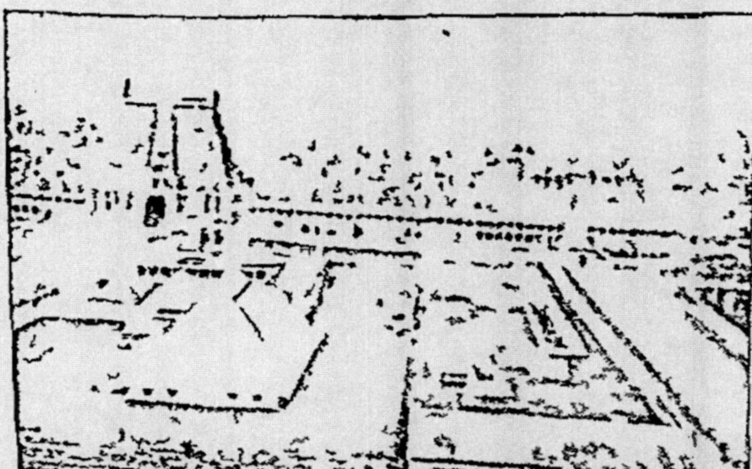

A General View of the Great Temple with the Southern Gopuram in the back ground

RAHU & KETU

(IN A NICHE OF THE EAST GOPURA—NORTH SIDE)

NARADA
(IN A NICHE OF THE EAST GOPURA)

AGASTYA

(IN A NICHE OF THE EAST GOPURA—EAST SIDE)

PATANJALI
(IN A NICHE OF THE EAST GOPURA)

KALYANASUNDARA AND SVYAMVARA
(EAST GOPURA—WEST SIDE)

GAJAHAMURTI

(IN A NICHE OF THE EAST GOPURA—EAST SIDE)

URDAVA THANDAVA

(IN A NICHE OF THE EAST GOPURA—NORTH SIDE)

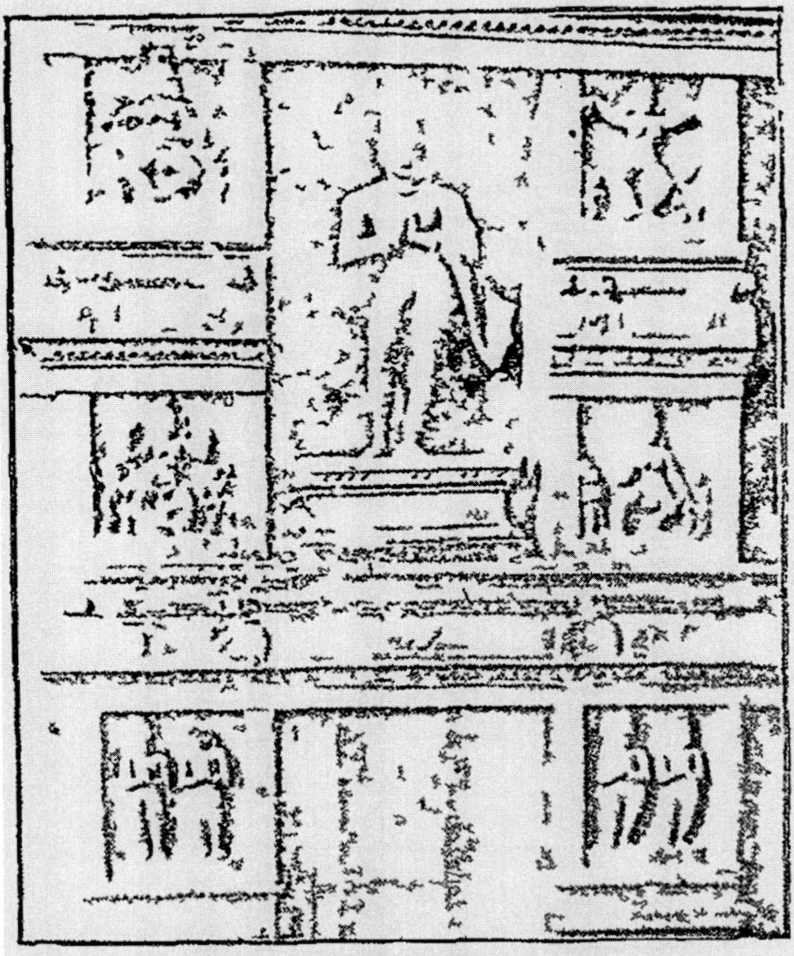

KRISHNADEVA RAYA
(NORTH GOPURA)

DURGA

(IN A NICHE OF THE NORTH GOPURA—SOUTH SIDE)

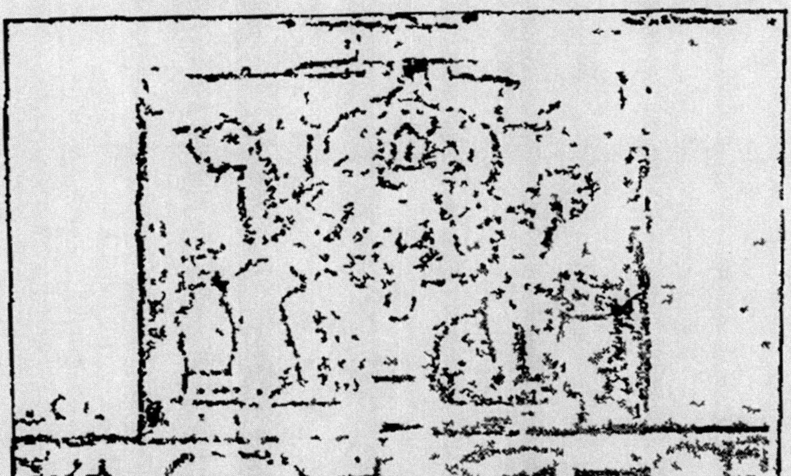

SIVA playing on a five-mouthed pot

(BASE OF THE NRITTA SABHA)

TRIPURĀNTAKAMŪRTI

PASUPATAMŪRTI

GANAPATI DANCING

(IN A PILLAR OF THE PORCH OF THE AMMAN TEMPLE)

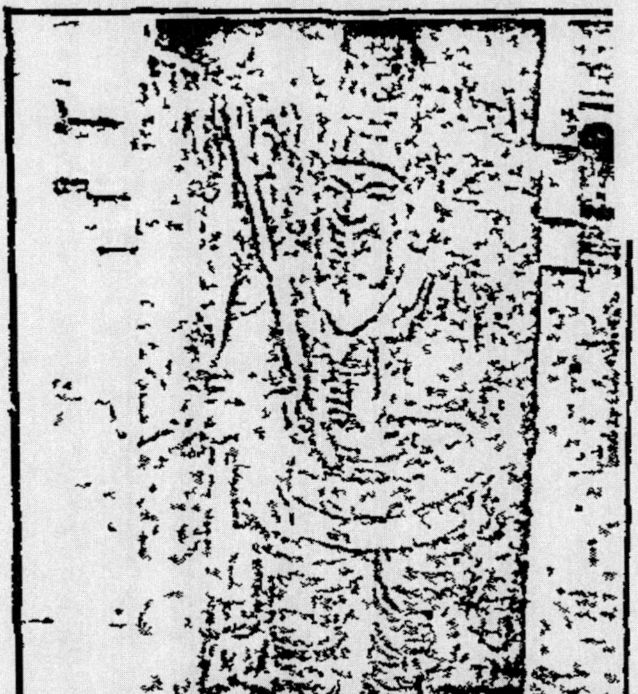

VYĀGHRAPĀDA